MW00748318

OVERWHELMED AGAIN

Discovering God's Comfort, Compassion, and Healing in the Midst of Mental Health Struggles

OVERWHELMED AGAIN

Peter Golin, MD &
Winnie Chung, PhD

Fedd Books
P.O. Box 341973
Austin, TX 78734
www.thefeddagency.com

Published in association with The Fedd Agency, Inc., a literary agency.

ISBN: 978-1-943217-70-0
eISBN: 978-1-943217-71-7

Printed in the United States of America
First Edition 15 14 13 10 09 / 10 9 8 7 6 5 4 3 2

“Praise be to the God and Father of our Lord Jesus Christ, the Father of compassion and the God of all comfort, who comforts us in all our troubles, so that we can comfort those in any trouble with the comfort we ourselves receive from God.”

— 2 Corinthians 1:3-4

TABLE OF CONTENTS

INTRODUCTION

What comes to mind when you hear the term "mental illness"? In the past, and perhaps even now in some circles, those who struggled with mental health problems were viewed as "crazy" or "scary." However, mental illness, mental disorders, disorders of the mind, or whatever term you choose, affects many, many of us. Human beings—created by God, loved, and *made in his very image*—experience deficiencies in mental health. Individuals across the nations, male or female, children or adults, likely have experienced anxiety, depressed mood, sleep problems, and many other symptoms of imperfect mental health in their normal, everyday lives. Mental health difficulties are more common than we might think, and those who struggle are in need of love, help, comfort, and healing.

A majority of us will not only experience symptoms of imperfect mental health but also suffer from diagnosable mental illnesses that affect our education, work, human relationships, and faith, which includes our worship and service within the church. Some of the more commonly discussed mental illnesses include the depressive disorders, anxiety disorders, bipolar disorders, eating disorders (including anorexia, bulimia, binge-eating disorder), and schizophrenia, but the list goes on. Other struggles experienced include addictive disorders (e.g., to alcohol, drugs, gambling), post-traumatic stress disorder (PTSD), obsessive-compulsive disorder (OCD), autism spectrum disorder, and attention-deficit/hyperactivity disorder (ADHD). According to the Center for Disease Control and Prevention (CDC), approximately 25 percent of adults in the United States have a mental illness, and almost 50 percent of adults will develop a mental illness in their lifetime.[1] Medical textbooks list *over 300* mental illness diagnoses. If you don't struggle with a mental illness, you likely know someone who does. We live, work, go to school, play sports, fellowship in church, and socialize daily with people who suffer from mental illness.

How about within the Christian church? It is likely that a significant number of people in your church is suffering from some form of mental illness. A recent study found that 59 percent of pastors surveyed had counseled at least one individual who was later diagnosed with a mental illness, and 23 percent of pastors reported they personally had experienced a mental disorder themselves.[2]

Unfortunately, mental health problems are frequently experienced in secret, with sufferers hoping no one will find out. Pastors and church leaders may often be unaware of the suffering their members go through. Leaders who do become aware may feel inadequate to help their flock due to lack of training, experience, and resources. These issues often lead to a referral to a medical professional such as a physician, psychiatrist, or psychologist who appropriately treats and cares for the sufferer.

But what about spiritual care and counsel? Many traditional and mainstream medical and psychological treatments for mental illness are effective and have a strong evidence base, but they are not sufficient for the Christian who is also seeking to understand *God's* view of their struggles. Is there a biblical, Christ-centered approach to managing mental health problems? We are convinced there needs to be.

As a Christian medical doctor and pastor for almost thirty years and Christian clinical psychologist, we, the authors, strongly believe that God, our creator, understands every mental health problem that exists and is the ultimate healer of each one of them. In addition to care received by medical professionals, medications, psychotherapy and counseling, natural herbs, and/or hospitalizations, the healing process of

Christians should *always* include God's wisdom found in the Holy Scriptures. Biblical spiritual truths are vital to the treatment and healing of mental illness.

Our aim in writing this devotional is to encourage and uplift individuals who experience various forms of mental illness. Far from trying to "fix" any problem, we simply offer daily readings and reflections to spur readers on in steadfast pursuit of the Lord in the midst of their mental health struggles. The daily readings intertwine God's Word from the Scriptures with personal experiences. Each personal word and Scriptural reflection is then followed by a prayer that we hope will encourage readers' own intimacy and communion with God. Then there is an "action item" that prompts readers to personalize and apply the written content in order to strengthen their individual faith and support their journey to improved mental health. Finally, readers are given a question to consider as they meditate on God's presence with them during the course of a mental illness. We hope each devotional will remind our brothers and sisters of our unfailing hope in the Lord Jesus and his faithful love, which carries us through the most seemingly hopeless of times.

Although this devotional is certainly not a book

of professional advice, it is unique in that it is written from the perspectives of a physician and pastor and clinical psychologist, both of whom are followers of Christ tasked with the work of making him known in their respective professional spheres. We hope this devotional will further bridge the gaps that are sometimes viewed to exist between spiritual, physical, and mental health, as well as reduce the stigma and fear of mental illness that may be held by some in the Christian church. In a similar vein, we trust this devotional can serve as a helpful resource for Christian leaders ministering to members in their congregation, equipping them with increased awareness of symptoms of mental illness and offering written material that can be compassionately shared with those experiencing mental health difficulties. We believe too that families and friends can offer these words to their loved ones, read and walk alongside them, and guide them in prayer for healing and help.

Finally, and most of all, we pray this devotional will honor the Lord Jesus, who has laid on our hearts the burning passion to reach the lost and the broken. Our desire is to minister to the sick and hurting with the love and power of God.

HOW THIS BOOK CAN BE USED

The following devotionals will take you on a journey through selected passages of Scripture, encouraging you as you walk through your mental health difficulties. The chosen verses, followed by prayers, suggestions for practical application, and personal reflection questions aim to help you gain victory and success in the treatment of your illness as seen from God's perspective.

Some of the contents of this book may be triggering, and this book has not been written to take the place of appropriate medical treatment by trained mental health professionals. We encourage seeking medical and psychological help and using this book as a spiritual guide alongside your prescribed treatment. This book can be read as:

- A daily devotional for adults and youth suffering from any form of mental health problem, offering encouragement, guidance, and comfort.
- A resource for pastors and church leaders as they counsel, support, and shepherd their

flocks.

- A resource for Christian mental health workers, including medical doctors, psychiatrists, psychologists, counselors, and nurses, as they treat their patients.
- A resource for all Christians who want to help their believing family members and friends through times of mental health struggles.
- A resource for Christians who want to share their faith in Jesus Christ with those suffering from any form of mental health difficulty.

OUR OPENING PRAYER FOR YOU

Dear Heavenly Father,

Thank you for the beloved individuals who are holding this book in their hands right now. We know they are created in your image, and we praise you that they are fearfully and wonderfully made by your own hands. Lord, you know more intimately and fully than anyone else the very struggles and pain they are experiencing, and we know that you care deeply about each of them. Be it a diagnosis of a mental disorder, a season of sadness and anxiety, a period of overwhelming stress and discontent, or a combination of the above and more, we ask for healing and restoration in the powerful name of Jesus. You are the ultimate healer of our emotional, mental, physical, and spiritual health.

We believe in faith, God, that you are able to do more than we could ever ask or imagine, so we pray that whether healing occurs instantaneously, over the course of weeks, months, and years, or throughout a lifetime, you would equip your children with strength, trust, and perseverance to stand firm in your truth no matter how dark the days and how long the nights. Help your children remember to seek your face always and know that your perfect love never fails. Please reach out your compassionate and powerful hand, touch their hearts, and restore the joy that may have been lost.

May you bring to life the words on the pages that follow, and may you awaken a fervent desire in all of us to know you more fully, love you more deeply, and trust you more completely. You are compassionate and merciful in all of your ways, and nothing—including mental illness—can separate your children from your love. May those who are overwhelmed by difficulties in their emotional, mental, physical, and spiritual health be now overwhelmed by your love, mercy, grace, comfort, compassion, and healing power.

Use this book for your glorious purposes, Lord God, and may you gently remind your precious children that even in their mental health struggles, you are near and walking with them every step of the way.

In the loving and powerful name of Jesus Christ we pray, amen.

ONE
EXHAUSTED

"God is light; in him there is no darkness at all. If we claim to have fellowship with him yet walk in the darkness, we lie and do not live by the truth. But if we walk in the light, as he is in the light, we have fellowship with one another, and the blood of Jesus, his Son, purifies us from all sin."

— 1 John 1:5-7

Today I am feeling particularly weary and exhausted. Every step I take feels so heavy and strenuous, and the mere thought of failing to overcome these temptations once again is leaving me so discouraged and disheartened. As much as I fully believe that the Lord has forever rescued me from the dominion of darkness, I can't help but realize that my patterns of behavior and thought resemble more a life lived in disobedience to God than one lived by the empowerment of the Holy Spirit and under the lordship of Christ. *Why* do I continue to engage in these fruitless and shameful actions time after time? *Why* is it so difficult to "put aside the deeds of darkness and put on the armor of light" (Romans 13:12)?

I suppose this is the reality of the power of sin. Gaining victory over the deeply entrenched sinful desires inside our bodies really isn't as simple as merely "shaking off" the temptations that come. We desperately need and depend on the power of our God to help us fight this fierce battle. "Jesus said, 'If you hold to my teaching, you are really my disciples. Then you will know the truth, and the truth will set you free'" (John 8:31-32). The truth of Jesus sets us free. He has died to release us from our deep bondage to sin so that we no longer have to stumble in the darkness of our wickedness. We can walk freely in the light of his mercy and grace.

Not all of our steps will be easy, but whenever and however we fall, our loving God, who is with us wherever we go, will always pick us up and continue helping us live in his light. Let's not forget that *Jesus Christ has already won the war with sin on our behalf.* Rejoice that we now stand free from condemnation before our righteous and loving God. We no longer belong to darkness, but are, in fact, beloved children of light.

PRAYER

Dear Heavenly Father,

I am discouraged and disheartened because of the shameful actions I perform in my sinful body. Please forgive me and purify me from all sin. You have forever rescued me from the power of sin. Jesus is my Lord, and the Holy Spirit is my source of power. The truth of your gospel has set me free from the power of Satan and hell. It is the blood of Jesus that purifies me from all sin. Teach me how to daily gain victory over my temptations and disobedient actions. Please help me trust in the work of Christ that was done on the cross for me, obey your commandments, and delight in Jesus. Hold me and show me how to walk in the light. In the precious and victorious name of Jesus, amen.

MOVING FORWARD:

- Memorize John 8:31-32: "Jesus said, 'If you hold to my teaching, you are really my disciples. Then you will know the truth, and the truth will set you free.'" Highlight this verse in your Bible.

- Do something today to take care of your body, which God has purified and freed from the bondage to sin and darkness. Take a leisurely walk, enjoy a warm bath, or light a nice-smelling candle, all the while reminding yourself of the freedom you have in Christ.

How convinced are you that as an adopted child of God, you now stand free from condemnation before your righteous and loving God? Do you believe you no longer belong to darkness, but are a beloved child of light?

TWO
HERE I GO AGAIN

"So, if you think you are standing firm, be careful that you don't fall!"
— 1 Corinthians 10:12

I can be even more anxious on good days than bad ones. I tell myself not to celebrate good moments so soon because I don't know what I might do or what might happen tomorrow, an hour from now, or even five minutes later. I remind myself of the agony and pain that accompanied my last "act of disobedience" and the likelihood of my engaging in these same sinful behaviors once again. I force myself to believe that it is impossible for me to stop performing these patterns of deeply ingrained behaviors because these habits are not so easily broken. However, my self-defeating attempts to "be careful that I don't fall" actually serve to jump-start my fall into those same despicable behaviors all over again.

Rather than desiring for us to live in constant fear

over the uncertainties of every new moment, I think God is intending to caution us against dismissive disregard for Satan's subtle, yet dangerous, schemes. We need to be mindful, but not constantly worried; vigilant, but not apprehensive; alert, but not anxious. How can we focus on keeping our feet firmly planted if our attention keeps bouncing from one anxious thought to another? How effective can we be in avoiding stumbling blocks if we are too busy planting our own hindrances? Clearly, we must be prayerfully diligent in preventing Satan from gaining a foothold, but I think our faith and trust in God's sure victories can grow tremendously if we sincerely thank the Lord as he helps us overcome each temptation and obstacle and praise him for every small victory, knowing that each triumph brings us closer to the final prize that he has already won for us.

PRAYER

Dear Heavenly Father,

On days when I feel like I am standing firm, help me to be careful that I don't fall. Thank you that you will never allow me to be tempted beyond what I am able to endure. Your Word promises me that you are faithful, and that with every temptation that comes my way, you will always provide me with a way of escape so that I may be able to endure the temptation. Please help me understand that even though Satan is always tempting me and trying to destroy me, you, my God, are for me, and you are greater than Satan and his evil schemes. I praise you, Lord, for every victory. Please replace my anxieties with your peace and complete trust in your power. In the name of Jesus, my provider, I pray, amen.

MOVING FORWARD:

- Write out your five greatest temptations—ones that you frequently fall under and which result in sin. Present them to God on a daily basis, asking him always to help you find a way of escape.

- Record the ways of escaping temptation that God has shown you. Commit to following the Lord's guidance when you face a temptation next.
- Combine prayer with fasting next time you are tempted for an extended period of time; it can be a powerful tool.

How does God provide a way of escaping and overcoming every temptation you encounter?

THREE
CAN I REALLY TRUST YOU?

"He answered their prayers, because they trusted in him."

— 1 Chronicles 5:20

Is it that simple? All we have to do is trust in the Lord, and our prayers will be answered? It certainly *sounds* simple, but it may not be so easy to do. What exactly happens when we pray? What does trusting in God actually mean?

We are told over and over again to commit and devote ourselves to prayer, presenting all kinds of requests to God and praying for all kinds of people. But if our Father already knows what we need before we ask, why do we have to bother asking?

Prayers accomplish more than simply making our needs known to God. Jesus promised that we would receive whatever we ask in his name, so clearly, earnest prayers can definitely effect amazing and even dramatic changes. Besides—and most importantly—

Jesus himself prayed. The act of praying can work something extraordinary in our hearts. As James 1:6 says, "But when he asks, he must believe and not doubt, because he who doubts is like a wave of the sea, blown and tossed by the wind." When we pray in the Spirit, the Lord can fill us with inexpressible peace and strength, giving us the incredible ability to trust that he is able to and will accomplish unimaginable deeds for us and on our behalf. He bestows upon us renewed faith to surrender all of ourselves into his sovereign and powerful hands and reveals to us the sureness and certainty of his promises.

God has answered countless prayers in the past, and he still answers prayers today. Eloquent words are hardly necessary, for I have every confidence that God hears even the faintest and softest "amen".

PRAYER

Dear Father,

I have prayed to you many times, asking that you would heal me from my illness. At times, it seems to me that you are not listening. Help me to continue to believe that you not only have the ability but also the desire to heal me. I pray that you would replace my doubts with greater faith. Teach me how to pray, and when I no longer have any words because of my great emotional pain, I ask that my advocate, the Holy Spirit, will carry my tears and groans before your throne. Today I choose to continue praying for my healing. I choose not to doubt, but to believe in the God who has created me in a very special way. Today I choose to trust God who answers the prayers of his children. I ask these things in the trusted name of Jesus, amen.

MOVING FORWARD:

- Read the following Scriptures on what it means to trust God: Proverbs 3:5-6 and Psalm 37:3-7. Commit yourself to memorizing Proverbs 3:5-6.

- Consider starting a prayer journal, listing the prayers you have offered to the Lord and recording the ways in which he has answered your requests. Review this journal periodically and remind yourself of God's faithfulness towards you. Thank him and praise him for his faithfulness.

What experiences have you had in your life that have affected your ability to trust God?

FOUR
DOES ANYBODY CARE?

"Look to the LORD and his strength;
seek his face always."
— 1 Chronicles 16:11

I don't quite understand why, but during my times of deep discouragement and sadness, even merely *seeing* a familiar and trusted face can give me that extra bit of strength and motivation to carry on another day. Perhaps it is the security and reassurance I feel in knowing that there is still at least one person in this world who may still care about me. Or perhaps, even though I feel all alone and abandoned, I am reminded of the ways in which I have felt loved and protected in the past. Whatever the reason, there is a strange sense of comfort that sweeps over me.

I have no doubt that ultimately, it is the glimpse of God that will equip me with all the strength I need to carry on for not just one more day, but for all the days he has in store for me. Somehow, seeking him and finding his face to be shining down on me can reignite the hope that is mine and awaken again the desire to live an obedient life that is pleasing to my Lord. I think of the lyrics to the encouraging old hymn by Helen Howarth Lemmel: "Turn your eyes upon Jesus, / Look full in his wonderful face. / All the things of earth will grow strangely dim / In the light of his glory and grace". This is what happens when we gaze upon the beauty of our Lord, isn't it? We can become so captured and overwhelmed by his glory that all our troubles slip away and fade into the background. When the center of our attention is fixed on God alone, nothing can shake us, nothing can move us, and nothing can crush us.

PRAYER

Dear Lord,

Help me today to concentrate on your beauty and your glory, rather than my struggles and difficulties. When I am in pain, help me to turn my eyes upon Jesus, to look full in his wonderful face. And when I do, may all the things of this earth, especially my emotional turmoil, grow strangely dim, in the light of your glory and grace. Teach me, God, how to seek your face always, how to find your face, how to recognize your face, and how to gain strength by looking into your face. Teach me, God, how to look for strength in you, my Lord and Savior, my King and my friend, my heavenly physician and healer. In the caring name of Jesus I pray, amen.

MOVING FORWARD:

- Read Revelation 4 and Revelation 19:11–16. Now lie down, close your eyes, and meditate on the images from these Scriptures. Imagine yourself being in the presence of God right now, looking at him face-to-face. Be amazed and comforted by what you see. You might even draw out what you imagine being in the presence of God.

How often do you use your imagination to picture yourself in God's presence—looking at him face-to-face, embracing him, holding his hand, crying on his shoulder, and laughing with him?

FIVE
HELPLESS WITH YOUR POWE.

"For the message of the cross is foolishness t
are perishing, but to us who are being saved
it is the power of God."
— 1 Corinthians 1:18

Isn't it amazing that because of the cross, we can not only taste the magnificence of God's power, but we can also experience the power of God acting *for us*, on *our* behalf? To realize that the power of the one who created everything out of nothing, who put in order all that was not, is working in our lives . . . that just astounds me and leaves me speechless. We must hold so dearly in our hearts the message of the cross because it is the power of God that strengthens and sustains us. And oh, how I need power! I know I cannot make it through the day without a fresh dose of God's empowerment minute by minute, hour by hour. If I could only see how helpless I truly am and how *utterly* dependent I am on my God, I would perhaps begin understand just how powerful his power really is.

It can be so easy to underestimate the power of God. I tend to lump everything that man *cannot* do into the "God's power" category, but I must realize that we are only able to do what we *can* do because of the power of God too. As Jesus said, "Apart from me you can do nothing" (John 15:5).

Today I want to rest in the power of God, relying wholly on him to help me bear my cross as I follow him home. I want to remember that "all that we have accomplished, [he] has done for us" (Isaiah 26:12). Let me never complain that I am lacking in strength and might, for although I am weak in myself, I am "strong in the Lord and in his mighty power" (Ephesians 6:10).

PRAYER

Dear Heavenly Father,

Help me place the cross and death of Jesus Christ in front of my eyes every day of my life. Help me see that the death of Jesus has not only saved me from eternal condemnation, but also allows me to receive forgiveness for my daily sins. Help me nail my mental illness onto this cross on a daily basis and see that the death of Jesus and the shedding of his blood give me forgiveness and healing. Today I accept the sacrifice of Jesus paid for me on that cross. It is a free gift given to me by Jesus, and I do not have to earn it. Although as a human being I am weak, as a child of God, I have received the power of God, so I will be strong in the Lord and in his mighty power. I acknowledge that without God I can do nothing. But with you, dear God, I am able to be healed from my physical, emotional, and mental disorders. I ask these things in the powerful name of Jesus, amen.

MOVING FORWARD:

- Draw a large cross on a poster. Hang it somewhere on a wall in your home where you can see it on a daily basis. On a small piece of paper, print your diagnosis, such as anxiety, eating disorder, bipolar disorder, obsessive-compulsive disorder, etc. and pin it to the cross.

- Whenever temptations associated with your mental illness arise, look to the poster and remind yourself that your specific mental health struggles have been nailed to the cross and that Jesus has paid the price to redeem all the brokenness that exists in this fallen world. By his stripes, we are healed (Isaiah 53:5).
- Put to memory and remind yourself daily of the biblical truth that all sins, whether committed during the course of a mental illness or any other time, have been paid for by Christ's death on the cross. Seek God's forgiveness for each of your sins on a daily basis.

How often do you try to earn forgiveness through some type of activity or by your own means? How can you increase your confidence that the death of Christ on the cross has completely accomplished the work needed to be done for the forgiveness of your sins and your salvation?

SIX
HELP ME REMEMBER

"Then Samuel took a stone and set it up between Mizpah and Shen. He named it Ebenezer, saying, 'Thus far has the LORD helped us.'"

— 1 Samuel 7:12

When times get tough, it is easy to forget God's loving concern for our lives and the guidance and direction he has provided for us in the past. I get so caught up in my present questioning and uncertainty of God's providence that I refuse myself the encouragement that comes from remembering all the marvelous deeds God has done for me. Furthermore, Satan tries to cause me to doubt God's faithfulness and lead me to believe that what I understand to be God's providential work is merely a delusion. Even in times when I can clearly see the sovereign hand of God working in my life and the lives of others, I overestimate my ability to remember and falsely believe that I would be able to recall these instances at a later time. I so easily forget, yet I *cannot* forget. "Only be careful, and watch yourselves closely so that you do not forget the things your eyes have seen or let them fade from your heart as long as you live" (Deuteronomy 4:9).

Throughout the Bible, God's children are continually reminded of the great deeds God has performed. We too need to always meditate on the wonderful acts of God. Clearly, his word provides us with many detailed descriptions of God's triumphs and victories, and regularly reading these historical accounts can serve as consistent reminders of his all-surpassing greatness. How else can we remember his unique work in our lives? Like Samuel, we can set up small "monuments" to symbolize the different ways God has provided for and spoken to us. Perhaps a journal entry, a painting, a poem, or a song can be a way by which we can remember our special encounters with God. Whatever method we may choose, we must remember.

PRAYER

Dear Lord,
Remind me today how you have helped me through my mental health problems, especially how you have provided me with good medical care—medication when I needed it, doctors, nurses, therapists, and perhaps even hospitalization. Remind me today of the financial support you provided through people such as my parents, my employer, my disability insurance, the government social welfare program, and the Christian church. Remind me today of how you have been faithful to me by protecting me from suicide and other forms of death. May your Holy Spirit remind me daily of your triumphs and victories in my life, especially relating to my mental health. Thank you for your love and providence. I pray these things in the precious name of Jesus, amen.

MOVING FORWARD:

- Create an "ugly sweater" similar to what people wear at Christmas. Call it a "Monument Sweater." Glue words on the sweater such as "God is faithful," "God is sovereign," "God is my provider," "God cares for me," "God is with me," "God is my Father," "God is my healer," and "God loves me." Wear or look at your sweater whenever Satan causes you to doubt God's providence and faithfulness. Wear or look at your sweater whenever you need to be encouraged. Add words and phrases to the sweater when God provides victories in your life. Encourage a friend who suffers from mental health problems to do the same.

What other practical methods can you use to help you remember God's blessings and faithfulness to you?

SEVEN
WHEN WILL YOU COME?

"Now I know in part; then I shall know fully, even as I am fully known."

— 1 Corinthians 13:12

With the advent of high-definition cameras and television, recorded images that we view of ourselves and celebrities are becoming clearer and even more life-like. But it is just not the same as seeing these same people face-to-face. The eyes, mouths, and noses are all there, but *something* is missing, isn't it? No matter how "high quality" the cameras really are, captured images can only very closely *resemble* the real thing.

Isn't this similar to our present knowledge of the Lord? Of course, the more we listen to him, talk with him, and read his Word, the greater our understanding of him becomes. But until that final day when we actually stand before him, seeing him face-to-face, touching his nail-pierced hands, we cannot know him as completely and absolutely as we want. There are so many questions I long to ask and so many words I desire to hear him speak, but I wonder if any of them will matter anymore once I see his glorious face. Somehow, I suspect that all my uncertainties and doubts will be fully satisfied and resolved with just one glance of him in all his glory.

After not seeing a friend for awhile, I tend to worry that somehow during our time apart he or she may have become upset with me for some reason, and lists of questions and worries start to develop in my mind. However, my anxieties are put to rest when we finally meet, for the warmth and kindness with which I am greeted assures me that no tension exists between us. While my desire to see the Lord does not stem from a fear of his anger, for I know that the wrath due me has been borne by Christ, I do have the same eagerness, if not greater, to look upon the face of God. I need him, and somehow, although I've never been to heaven, I miss my eternal home.

The good news is that Christ *is* coming, despite how long this waiting seems to last. "He who testifies to these things says, 'Yes, I am coming soon.' Amen. Come, Lord Jesus" (Revelation 22:20).

PRAYER

Dear Savior,
I eagerly long for the day when I will see you face-to-face—when you will hold me, when you will wipe away all my tears. Right now, I have so many questions to ask you, so many uncertainties and doubts, so many anxieties about my life and my health, but I do believe that when I meet you, you will fulfill my every need. I thank you that even in my imperfect condition, you are making yourself known to me. I am coming to understand you, love you, and know you more through my weaknesses. Come quickly, Lord Jesus, come quickly. In the name of Jesus, my soon-coming King, amen.

MOVING FORWARD:

- Knowing all of the names given to Jesus in the Bible helps us understand more fully who Jesus truly is. Identify some names of Jesus given in the Bible and study their meaning. Here are a few to help you get started: Lord, Savior, Christ, Rose of Sharon, Lily of the Valley, Holy, Messiah, Lamb of God, Shepherd, and

Bread of Life. See how many more you can add to that list. Call upon him as you wait in great anticipation for his second coming.

Which of the names given to Jesus is most meaningful to you in your present state of mental health and as you look forward to his return?

EIGHT
JEALOUS

"You shall not covet your neighbor's house."

— Exodus 20:17

I may not covet anybody's *house* per se, but I can become very jealous of other people's *lives*. Have you ever met people who seem to be loved by everyone? I am jealous of them. Then there are the many individuals who do not struggle in the same ways I do. I am jealous of them. I should, of course, be thankful that they are not experiencing the same kinds of suffering as I am, yet much of what I feel is jealousy. When successes come their way, I know I should be genuinely happy for them, but somehow, I cannot. I am just plain jealous.

"You are still worldly. For since there is jealousy and quarreling among you, are you not worldly? Are you not acting like mere men?" (1 Corinthians 3:3). How can I continue to live as if I am of the world, since it has already been crucified to me and I to it

(Galatians 6:14)? Through the cross of Jesus, I am no longer bound to the vain desires of the world, but rather am free to pursue the righteous and purpose-filled life that my Lord has purchased for me. When will I stop seeking more than what God says is enough? When will I learn to be *content* with the portion he has granted me for this time in my life? There is so much I cannot control and so much I cannot choose, but God faithfully provides everything I need.

I so often long for things to be *different*. If only I could wake up tomorrow morning with an unwavering conviction that people do love me. If only I could instantaneously overcome these struggles. If only, if only, if only . . . If only I would truly trust the Lord in every single aspect of my life with every last bit of my heart, then there would be no more "if onlys." I would then be content, and I would find that because I have *God*, I really do have more than enough.

PRAYER

Dear God,

Forgive me for being jealous of other people's lives, wanting what they have and who they are. I am sometimes jealous, and that is sin. I am often not content with my life and the burden of carrying my health problems. I often see others, who seem undeserving, being blessed by you, and that creates in me feelings of jealousy and anger. Lord, please teach me to be content and not jealous, heavenly-minded and not worldly. Help me to pursue the righteous and purpose-filled life you have purchased for me. Help me to be thankful and not grumbling so that your true peace can be found in me. I don't want to be a hypocrite, claiming to want only what you want for me, yet secretly desiring what the world has to offer with an attitude of jealousy. May your Holy Spirit remind me every day that I have been crucified with Christ, and that it is not I who live, but Christ who lives in me. I pray these things in the name of Jesus, my all in all, amen.

MOVING FORWARD:

- Be completely honest and write down three

to five things you are jealous of: good looks, money, good mental health, healthy marriages, an excellent job, a beautiful home, a fancy car, a beautiful singing voice, wonderful parents, obedient children, etc.

- Now write down three to five things you have that others might be jealous of: a home, daily food, freedom to worship God without persecution, a caring church, Christian friends, affordable medications, caring doctors, counselors and nurses, salvation by grace through Christ, clean running water and reliable electricity, the Bible, affordable education, democracy, etc.
- Present both of your lists to the Lord in a humble and prayerful attitude, giving him thanks. Repeat today's devotional prayer. Do this daily and pay attention to how the Lord changes your heart.

What might daily repentance look like for you and how might you do this?

NINE
WHY ME?

"Don't you know that you yourselves are God's temple and that God's Spirit dwells in your midst?"

— 1 Corinthians 3:16

There are moments when a particular passage of Scripture "jumps out" at me. Words I have become so familiar with all of a sudden seem to take on whole new meanings. Does this not so clearly show that the Word of God truly is *active* and that the Lord *continues* to speak to us through his Scriptures as we delve into them day after day? Somehow God has a way of tugging at specific strings in my heart at the most fitting times, encouraging me, rebuking me, reminding me, and lifting me up. And I know he does the same for all of us who seek his Word and his wisdom, for "if you call out for insight and cry aloud for understanding, and if you look for it as for silver and search for it as for hidden treasure, then you will understand the fear of the LORD and find the knowledge of God"

(Proverbs 2:3-5).

I know that the Spirit of God dwells in me, but this truth really "hit me hard" as I came across it today. The Spirit of the God of the universe, of all creation, of my heart and soul, *lives in me*. How unfathomable! As difficult as it has been for me to believe that I am not an insignificant and unlovable creature, I am simply baffled that God himself would choose *my* life as that which he would save and as that in which he would dwell. Objectively, this clearly alters the entire course of my life as he lovingly works his wonders in and through me. The way by which I view my worth as a child of God must unquestionably change as well, though. I recently heard a song by Jonny Diaz, whose lyrics the Lord used to strike a special chord in my heart: "You were made to fill a purpose that only you could do / So there could never be a more beautiful you". We are beautiful because we have been created by, and in the image of, our most beautiful God, and he has created each of us with a uniqueness no one can imitate or replace. Because of this, there truly cannot be a more beautiful *you*, or a more beautiful *me*. We are loved exactly the way we are.

PRAYER

Dear God,

Thank you for living inside my body. Despite all my physical, emotional, and mental difficulties, you have chosen to live in me forever. You chose me, found me, and saved me. Your Holy Spirit has entered into my soul and given me new birth. I am now a new creature in Christ. The old has passed away, and since my spiritual birth, all things are new. This means that you love my body, for you would never choose to live in my body if you did not love it. You do not choose perfect bodies to dwell in, for no perfect bodies exist. Thank you for living in my body, for taking care of my body, mind, and soul, and for understanding all of the needs that my body has. Please help me take good care of this body that you reside in. In the name of Jesus, my sovereign Lord, amen.

MOVING FORWARD:

- God has given each of us the responsibility of looking after our bodies. This includes not smoking, not taking illegal drugs, eating in healthy ways, exercising regularly, getting sufficient sleep, visiting a good doctor regularly and following his or her advice. Find one area of health you need to focus on.

- Make a decision today to put your good desire into action, such as starting an exercise program, joining a gym, hiring a personal trainer, or joining a smoking cessation program. Discuss your plan with your doctor.

How is your life different as you accept God's truth that your body belongs to God and has been given to you for a short period of time on earth for his glory?

TEN
BURDENS TOO HEAVY

"Carry each other's burdens, and in this way you will fulfill the law of Christ."
— Galatians 6:2

Although I am surrounded by wonderful individuals who sincerely express their desire to help "carry my burdens", I still feel like I would rather keep my burdens all to myself. After all, my burdens are heavy enough already—I hardly want to burden anyone else with them. Conversely, what if what I feel as heavy burdens are in reality so light that "normal people" would laugh at my inability to triumph over weaknesses that are easily overcome by others? But we aren't commanded to only carry each other's "heavy" burdens, or the "big" burdens, or the "most difficult" burdens; however tough or easy our burdens may subjectively seem to us, we are told to carry them for one another.

But how do I help ease another person's struggles

when I already feel unable to handle my own? Perhaps there is more to bearing each other's burdens than to simply relieve and lighten their load. Perhaps our own burdens can diminish as we faithfully and lovingly encourage and care for the needs of our brothers and sisters. As we willingly open our arms to take hold of the heaviness that weighs down our fellow strugglers, might our own burdens not begin to quietly slip out of our anxiously clenched fists? Maybe through the process of bearing one another's burdens and witnessing the faithful work of God in every situation, we can gain renewed hope and courage to face our own unique battles. Without a doubt, the pure joy that comes from living in obedience to the Lord supplies us with more strength than we can fathom, so let us follow his perfect commands and instructions, reaching out to our struggling friends with the beautiful love of Christ.

PRAYER

Dear God,

You are fully aware of all the burdens I carry each day and how I struggle with them. They are becoming part on my being, and I have difficulty sharing them with others, even with those who are willing to help me. I don't know how to let go of some of them because I am ashamed, scared, proud, and disappointed. Please send me someone who I can share my burdens with. Also send me someone who I can help. Use me, with the spiritual gifts you have given me and my experiences of pain and hurt, to help carry the burdens of at least one person. As I help others, give me the courage to lay my burdens at your merciful feet and let go of them, putting my trust fully in your sovereign will. As I reach out to my struggling friends with the beautiful love of Christ, may you fill me with an even greater portion of your love, mercy, and grace. I pray this in the merciful name of Jesus, the carrier of my burdens, amen.

MOVING FORWARD:

- Write out a list of three to five burdens that are weighing heavily on your life.

- Write out a list of two to three people who you believe could carry some of those burdens.
- Pray and plead to God to give you the opportunity and courage to ask at least one of these people for help.
- Now ask God for him to provide you with one person who you can help.
- Call this person and encourage them with your willingness to lighten their burden.

When was the last time you had the opportunity and joy of helping someone with their burden, and how did it feel to see them blessed by your actions when you did it for the glory of God?

ELEVEN
SECRET SHAME

"He will bring to light what is hidden in darkness and will expose the motives of men's hearts."

— 1 Corinthians 4:5

It is said that there is a "secret side" to everybody that no one else sees. I cringe when I imagine the day when all that I have stuffed away and hidden will be brought into his glorious light. I try so hard to conceal those deficient parts of me, but as my sins and shortcomings pile and accumulate, I fear even now that they will begin to spill out, and I will be shamefully exposed. I think many people hold mistaken beliefs of me as being the "good girl" who rarely breaks the rules. If only they knew. If only they knew the dreadful thoughts that churn and stir in my mind, the detestable actions that are committed behind the privacy of a shut door, or the negative attitudes that lurk behind polite smiles . . . people may very well be surprised. What is unbeknownst to them, though, is not unbeknownst to God. This is perhaps why I shudder at the future when all will be laid bare.

But it will be alright. It will be alright because God will make all things right. He has seen the messiness and filthiness of my soul but has chosen to love me and save me all the same. Despite the discomfort of standing completely unprotected by my disguises and coverings before the Lord, when we have been wrapped with immortality and clothes that cover our shameful nakedness, our pain will be no more. When we finally meet the Lord face-to-face, our darkness will be completely engulfed by his light, and there will be no more need for hiding or concealing.

PRAYER

Heavenly Father,

I thank you that there is now no condemnation for those who are in Christ Jesus. I confess every one of my sins before you, believing and knowing that you will forgive me. I plead for your mercy and grace. Your Word promises me that if I confess my sins, you are faithful and just to forgive me of my sins and cleanse me from all unrighteousness. Thank you that when you forgive me, you also cleanse me, and I stand before you as if I have never sinned. The filth of my life has been thoroughly washed away because you have forgiven me. Teach me to repent of my sins quickly, knowing that you are my loving heavenly Father who is quick to forgive. I ask these things in the merciful and gracious name of Jesus, amen.

MOVING FORWARD:

- Today and in the days ahead, ask God to forgive you as soon as you have sinned. Do this quickly, honestly, sincerely, and confidently, knowing that God is full of mercy for his children. Confess your sins to God several times per day. Confessing your sins in the shower or bath is a good reminder that when God forgives us, he washes our filth away.

What is one hidden, sinful part of your life that you have never confessed to the Lord?

TWELVE
TEMPTED

"And God is faithful; he will not let you be tempted beyond what you can bear. But when you are tempted, he will also provide a way out so that you can endure it."

— 1 Corinthians 10:13

Despite knowing that God will not let me face any temptation beyond that which I can bear, I continually express my disappointment with God each time I fall prey. When I am unable to fight against temptations that God has fully equipped me to conquer, I still attempt to place the blame on God for not helping me overcome. Still, I must not forget that God unceasingly protects me from my greatest temptation, the temptation to completely dismiss God. I have fallen again and again to various temptations, but each one has thrown me harder on my knees and led me to more earnest and fervent prayer. With each failure, I am thrown deeper and deeper into the arms of God, gaining a stronger awareness of my utter dependence on his grace and strength. Perhaps this diminishing of self-reliance is the foundation for all triumphs over temptations. Perhaps God is building me up and strengthening me to stand more firmly in the face of temptation.

Until we accept by faith that *God* holds the ultimate power over all temptations, and he alone is able to keep us standing under their crushing power, we cannot fully appreciate the amazing gift God has purchased for us: the gift of total freedom and liberty from sin. On our own, we will surely fail, but by the grace of God, we can stand firmly and solidly no matter how strong the winds of temptation may blow. So let our spirits be heartened and let us rejoice, for in Christ we find the path to absolute victory over temptation and sin.

PRAYER

Dear God,

With every one of my failures, I am thrown deeper into your loving arms, where I gain a stronger awareness of my utter dependence on your grace, your strength, and your love. You came to save the lost and heal the sick. Jesus, you came to save and heal me. Please save me, please heal me, and when I give in to temptation, please forgive me. As I face every temptation, please help me look for and find the way of escape. I am in desperate need of your help. I plead these things in the forever-loving name of Jesus my Lord, amen.

MOVING FORWARD:

- Memorize 1 Corinthians 10:13: "No temptation has overtaken you except what is common to man. And God is faithful; he will not let you be tempted beyond what you can bear. But when you are tempted, he will also provide a way out so that you can endure it."
- Remind yourself that with every temptation and each time you fall short, God is faithful

and will renew your spirit and your mind. He has forgiven our every failure by his own blood and has erased all of our sin.

When you fall prey to temptation, how do you respond? Do you run away from God, fearing his wrath and punishment, or run towards your loving and forgiving Heavenly Father, acknowledging his grace and mercy?

THIRTEEN
IMPERFECT IN AN IMPERFECT WORLD

"For we know in part and we prophesy in part, but when completeness comes, what is in part disappears."
—1 Corinthians 13:9-10

Sometimes I forget that we are imperfect people living in an imperfect world. Sometimes I forget that the perfection I so long for will not come for a little while yet. I see all around me such unmistakable evidence of our fallen condition, and my heart pleads even more fervently for the Lord to come and restore all things *soon.* I see so many distressing events that *shouldn't* happen, I hear so many hurtful words that *shouldn't* be spoken, I know of so many actions that *shouldn't* be done. I suppose that the longing for an ideal, flawless life is a special gift that God has placed in our hearts, for it reminds us of the temporal nature of the present world, draws our attention away from the fleeting joys and strife of the present, and turns our hearts toward the eternal dwelling place he is preparing for us.

I am frequently told that I have unbelievably high expectations about many things, and I suspect that people are right about that. I see so many imperfections in and around me, and my natural inclination is to do all that I can to correct them, change them, and make them perfect as they were created to be. But that is not my role. Yes, we have the responsibility of keeping one another accountable to the commands of the Lord and to gently admonish each other when we see hearts wandering away from the truth, but the only one who can make perfect the imperfect is our *perfect God himself*. For now, let's love each other just as we are, forgiving each other, accepting each other, and treating each other as fellow beloved creations of God.

PRAYER

Dear Heavenly Father,

I know that I am imperfect living in an imperfect world. One day, when I am in heaven with you, in my glorified state, I will be perfect just as you are perfect. For now, help me to love all those around me just as they are, accepting them, forgiving them, and treating them as fellow beloved creations of God. Help me accept my parents as they are, my siblings as they are, my spouse as he or she is, my fellow students and coworkers as they are, other Christians as they are, and my friends as they are. I pray that I would not be the one to try to change them, but would instead let you change them to be more like Jesus Christ. In the name of the perfect God, Jesus, amen.

MOVING FORWARD:

- Make a specific point *not* to pray that God changes others, but that God would work on changing you.
- Pray that God would use the strengths and weaknesses of other people to improve your deficiencies.

- As you read the Bible and see weaknesses in your own life, ask God to transform you into the character of Christ.

What are some of your greatest weaknesses and struggles—fear, worry, anxiety? Do you spend more time looking for weaknesses in others or finding your own weaknesses and presenting them before the Lord? Why do you think that is?

FOURTEEN
PERFECTLY CLEAN

"But you were washed, you were sanctified, you were justified in the name of the Lord Jesus Christ and by the Spirit of our God."

— 1 Corinthians 6:11

I love penguins. I think what attracts me about them, other than their cuteness, is how *clean* they often look. I think they may owe their spanking white bellies to the pristine, clean snow they glide and travel upon. Any dirt or dust that may find their way onto these birds would surely be wiped away as they swoop and swoosh their way around their home.

Somehow, the cleanness of these delightful creatures reminds me of the beautiful truth of God's work in cleansing us completely from the guilty stain of our sins. "'Come now, let us settle the matter,' says the LORD. 'Though your sins are like scarlet, they shall be as white as snow; though they are red as crimson, they shall be like wool'" (Isaiah 1:18). It truly is an amazing image, isn't it? All the dust of our wickedness and the sand of our worries and cares has been washed away by the flowing blood of Christ. We now stand justified before the living God, freed from the chains of death, which were once so powerful to bring us down.

When I recall the many sins I continually commit and the many deficiencies I see in me, I am often filled with incredible guilt and shame. But I must remember that my soul has been thoroughly washed by Jesus' saving blood. I am forever clean, infinitely cleaner than even those adorable little penguins.

PRAYER

Dear God,

My mental illness sometimes causes me to feel incredible guilt and shame. But I believe that the blood of Jesus Christ shed on the cross for my sins has justified me and liberated me from the chains of death. According to your Word, I am now being washed and sanctified. No mental illness is able to stop the process of your sanctification. Your Holy Spirit is more powerful than my mental illness, my deficiencies, and the guilty stain of my sins. My mental illness is not a sin but an illness, a deficiency of my mind and body. When you bring me to heaven, I will stand before you in a glorified body with no mental or physical deficiency. Help me to trust in you and your promises. In the sanctifying name of Jesus, I pray, amen.

MOVING FORWARD:

- As you pray, close your eyes and picture yourself in heaven one day, in the presence of God, with no mental and physical deficiency. As you imagine that picture, repent of your sins, thank him, and worship him. In light of eternity, that time will be very soon.

- Write down as many of your mental and physical deficiencies that you can think off on a white board or black board, or on a piece of paper in pencil. Now erase them. Imagine that clean board or paper in heaven. This is the promise of God to all of his children.

When was the last time you imagined yourself completely whole, without sin, and without any mental and physical illness, and how did that make you feel?

FIFTEEN
BEYOND THIS PAIN

"Jabez cried out to the God of Israel, '. . . Let your hand be with me, and keep me from harm so that I will be free from pain.' And God granted his request."

— 1 Chronicles 4:10

The pain-avoidance instinct that seems so "normal" just may be a bit lost and too well-hidden in me. Are we not supposed to naturally feel inclined to stop a bleeding wound and strive to keep ourselves from harm? Then why do I sometimes desire to do the exact opposite, wishing for harm to come upon me instead?

It is by his love and grace that the Lord is allowing me to see and recognize the problems with my attraction to pain. We are taught in the Scriptures of God's plans and promises to protect his children from harm, so for me, to welcome and even *seek* harm in my life is clearly not what the Lord desires. But sometimes the emotional pain I experience is so intense and deep that inflicting physical pain upon myself seems like a "good" solution.

I need to remember that in the same way physical pain can't be relieved by creating emotional pain, we also can't fight emotional pain with physical pain. The Lord does not desire for me to inflict harm upon myself the way I do. He is the God who desires to keep us from all harm and who promises us a future in heaven that is free from all pain.

How though, can I endure for the time being? We are powerless to lighten the weight of our burdens or ease our sufferings by ourselves, but we can and must rely on the *Lord* to heal us completely, in every way. Sure, our suffering in one form or another will continue so long as we're living in our fallen bodies in this fallen world, but we need to trust that God can use our deepest hurts to accomplish his beautiful, God-glorifying purposes in us and in the world. So until that final day when our absolute deliverance will take place, let's keep holding tightly onto the hand of our Savior, knowing that because of his great love for us, we are equipped with more than enough strength and power to endure and overcome the pain of this world.

PRAYER

Dear Heavenly Father,

I am weak, but you are strong. I know I cannot overcome my emotional pain by inflicting physical pain upon myself. You desire no pain at all for me. Give me your strength to protect me from hurting myself physically. You have the power to lighten the weight of my burden. Please ease my suffering as I rely on you completely to heal me. I trust that in my deepest hurts you will accomplish your beautiful, God-glorifying purposes in my life. Heavenly Father, help me to keep holding tightly onto your hand, knowing that because of your great love for me, you have equipped me with more than enough strength and power to endure and overcome the pain of this world. Dear Lord, let your hand be with me, and keep me from harm so that I will be free from pain. I trust that you will grant my request. In the healing name of Jesus, amen.

MOVING FORWARD:

- Learn to cry out to the Lord with all your heart, all your mind, all your soul, and all your strength.

- Find a safe place where nobody can hear you, and cry out to God with all your strength and might. Scream and cry like you have never done before. Let your anger, despair, pain, frustration, and fear be expressed to God, your heavenly Father, in a loud voice and in the flowing of your tears.

When did you last cry out to the Lord, and how did it feel?

SIXTEEN
I LOVE YOU . . . I THINK?

"Dear children, let us not love with words or speech but with actions and in truth."

— 1 John 3:18

It sometimes amazes me how often we mindlessly and carelessly throw around the word *love*. Oh of course, many times we say it with all sincerity from a genuine heart, but aren't there times when the word is said out of obligation or merely established routine? Perhaps we want to convince ourselves that we do, in fact, love a certain individual, maybe we fear the consequences that may result if we *don't* speak the word, or maybe we've forgotten the actual significance of all that is conveyed by the words, "I love you".

Day after day, I tell the Lord that I love him with all my heart—more than anything or anyone else that exists—but do I really? Certainly I want to, but just how far do I fall short? Do my actions actually reflect what I claim? If I really loved God that much, am I completely willing to endure anything he would have me go through, trusting him fully with all my pain and uncertainties? Do I never doubt, for even a moment, that all his promises hold true in every situation, and that my struggles really are light and momentary in comparison to his eternal glory?

No, I doubt. And I want to give up. And I question his ability to save me from my sorrows. I want to love God so much more than that, but I struggle. I want to truly surrender every single part of my life and being to the Lord. I want my actions to consistently reflect what it truly means to love the Lord my God with all of my heart, mind, and soul. So I will work to love, not merely with words or tongue, but with convincing actions and in truth as well.

PRAYER

Dear Lord,

I say I truly love you, but today, I am not completely sure. Help me to understand that your love for me is perfect, but my love for you grows as I get to know you and trust you more and more each day. Help me to realize that my love for you grows particularly stronger during my trials and tribulations—like right now, in a period of deep depression. I am learning to understand how much you care for me. Help me, God, to fall in love with you more and express my love to you through prayer, worship in song and music, an attitude of thanksgiving, and complete obedience to your commandments. I am willing to endure my illness, knowing that you have a special plan for my life. In the name above all other names, Jesus, amen.

MOVING FORWARD:

- Let the first words from your mouth every morning be, "Dear Jesus, I love you. Teach me today to love you even more."
- Listen to what the Lord tells you as he shares ways to love him more fully than the day be-

fore, and keep reminding yourself of these revelations throughout the day.

- Do this daily for the next week, and see if you can make it a good daily habit.

When you think of loving God with words, actions, attitudes, and thoughts, which ones are most difficult for you?

SEVENTEEN
YOU KNOW IT ALL

"For God is greater than our hearts, and he knows everything."

— 1 John 3:20

I cannot bear to have others know things about me that I haven't willingly disclosed. In many ways, I desire to precisely control what others know of me or think of me. If they somehow find out about a sinful deed I have done or a personal flaw I have tried so hard to conceal, I can be filled with great shame and anger.

But there is something very different about *God* knowing my deepest troubles and shortcomings. I am relieved and thankful that he knows the secrets of my heart. The Lord knows me much more thoroughly than I even know myself, so it would be quite silly to attempt to hide *any*thing from him. I think my "comfort" in confessing to him my most horrible sins exists because my relationship with the Lord is incomparable to and vastly unlike my relationships with any other person I know. God gives me complete confidence that he loves me no matter what, forgives me no matter what, and will not be shocked or taken aback by whatever I may reveal to him. He already knows everything there is to know about me, yet still accepts me and welcomes me into his presence at any time, so there need not be even a slight hesitation for me to pour out my inmost concerns and failings to him.

What a gift this acceptance truly, truly is. I cannot grasp how God would allow me this privilege of enjoying such an intimate relationship with him. What astonishing grace. What amazing love. How *great* is our God!

PRAYER

Dear God,

You know everything about me, including my past, present, and future. You welcome me as your child into your presence at any time. There is nothing I can tell you about myself that would shock you. Yet knowing me so intimately—even the shameful parts—you continue to love me with an everlasting love. You pour out your kindness, grace, and mercy on me every day, despite my failures and sins. You are greater than my heart, greater than my anxiety and depression, greater than all my illnesses, and greater than my sins. Thank you for your amazing love. In the name of Jesus, the one who is all-knowing, amen.

MOVING FORWARD:

- Stand in front of a large mirror. You may not like everything about what you see. Remind yourself that God knitted every part of you intentionally, lovingly, and carefully. Remind yourself that God can also see the depths of your soul. He can read your thoughts, he knows your deepest feelings, and he understands your pain. He can see your physical and emotional scars, and still he loves you perfectly, forever.

What makes it difficult for you to be willing and ready to reveal to God all of what he already knows, including your fears, harmful behaviors and thought patterns, and shame?

EIGHTEEN
AM I LOVED?

"This is love: not that we loved God, but that he loved us and sent his Son as an atoning sacrifice for our sins."

— 1 John 4:10

I yearn so much to be loved, and I often work hard to try and earn that love. But isn't love something that is freely given rather than earned? It isn't hard to imagine that acting in "lovely" ways may very well breed affection from others, and not acting in agreeable ways would expectedly generate dislike from people. But *love*, *true* love, endures *all* things and extends to both the lovely and the unlovable. Of course, we should not deliberately act in aversive ways, and I suppose some people might seem easier to love than others, but whether or not we are loved ultimately doesn't depend on how we behave or act. In fact, love actually has very little to do with us, the beloved, at all. True love speaks more about the *one* who loves.

Love does not always come to us spontaneously

or easily; it is a choice we continually have to make. We have only been made able to sacrificially love God and our neighbors because *God* first loved us. One thing that amazes me about God's love is that he loved us and loves us despite our frequently rebellious and doubtful hearts against him. How could we ever love God as he deserves?

The fact that God loves us brings glory to him, not us. But in loving us, he promises us an eternal glory that far outweighs what we have ever known or experienced. And honestly, how else can we respond to this amazing love but to love Him in return?

PRAYER

Dear God,

Your love for me is amazing. You proved your love for me by dying on a cross while I was still an unsaved sinner. Now, as your child, you promise to love me with an everlasting love. Your love for me is constant even when my love for you, others, and myself is weak and cold. You promise to love me when I'm healthy and when I'm ill, when I like myself and when I hate myself, when I overcome temptation and when I fall prey to temptation, when my mental health struggles are particularly intense and when I am stable, when I feel happy and even when I am feeling suicidal. Teach me to love you and others in the same way that you love me. I pray this in the name of my loving Savior, Jesus, amen.

MOVING FORWARD:

- Ask God to bring to your mind someone you don't love very well at this particular time: a parent, spouse, sibling, child, friend, etc. Write them a short letter telling them that you love them and God loves them. Allow love to be a decision rather than merely a feeling. As you write the letter, ask God to fill you with true feelings of love for that person. If possible, follow-up after the letter with an *act* of love, such as sending a small gift or doing a kind deed.

When was the last time you thanked God for loving you, and when was the last time you thanked certain special people in your life for loving you?

NINETEEN
ALL BUT GIVEN UP

"Let us not become weary in doing good, for at the proper time we will reap a harvest if we do not give up."

— Galatians 6:9

I feel so ready to give up. Day after day, I wake up covered by the same veil of dread, confusion, and defeat, thinking with apprehension of yesterday's failures and the likelihood of them occurring again today. I feel so frightened about being stuck in this seemingly never-ending cycle and the eventual outcomes and consequences that may come to pass. It is becoming increasingly difficult for me to see any possibility for an "end" to these struggles.

If you've ever observed what happens when a speck of dust gets sucked in by a vacuum, you may have noticed that when the vacuum first approaches the dust, the pull is slight, and the piece of dust barely moves. But as the vacuum comes closer and closer, all of a sudden, the piece of dust accelerates and disappears inside it. I feel like the "vacuum" is getting ever so close to me. I feel like I am always on the brink of being completely sucked in. My resistance against the pull of despair is wearing out with each failure, so much so that sometimes giving up fighting and allowing myself to be pulled in seems like a good idea.

In the midst of this, I know that despite the wrong or harmful things I do every day, simply by persevering, trying to get through another day, and trying to walk closely with the Lord, I am actually able to please him. I may, in fact, be "doing good". I really don't see an achievable end to all this pain, but maybe I simply don't know when the proper end is. You know, we speak of "giving up" to mean "not trying anymore" or "admitting defeat", but if I so desire to give up, how about I give it all up to God? How about I completely yield, surrender, relinquish all control, and submit everything to him? Being conquered or overpowered by anything or anyone other than God is sure to engender feelings of hopelessness, but when it is God who is taking over, I am guaranteed to be empowered and strengthened. More than that, I am guaranteed *victory*, for he is on my side, and he always wins.

PRAYER

Dear God,

I feel like giving up. I am tired of fighting my daily battles. I often think of my previous failures and anticipate the likelihood of them occurring again. I'm ready to give up this seemingly never-ending cycle of sin, battles with depression, anxiety, insomnia, fear, emotional pain, and self-harm. Today I have decided to give it all up to you. I have chosen to admit defeat and fully surrender, completely yield, relinquish all control, and submit everything to you, Lord Jesus. I'm not sure what that all means, but according to your promises, I am guaranteed to be empowered and strengthened. As your Word promises, I am guaranteed victory, for you are on my side, and you always win. Now, as you take control of my life, help me not become weary in doing good, believing that in your proper time I will reap a good harvest. As you carry me in your hands, help me never to give up holding on to you. I pray these things in the victorious name of Jesus, amen.

MOVING FORWARD:

- Read and consider memorizing Matthew 16:24-25 in order to understand what it means to fully surrender your life to Christ: "Then Jesus told his disciples, 'Whoever wants to be my disciple must deny himself and take up his cross and follow me. For whoever would save his life will lose it, but whoever loses his life for me will find it. For what will it profit a man if he gains the whole world and forfeits his soul? Or what shall a man give in return for his soul?'" (Matthew 16:24-26).

What comes to mind when you spend time meditating on the phrases "deny yourself," "take up your cross daily", "follow Jesus", and "lose your life"? How does obeying these words help you "give up" and "give in" to the loving will of God?

TWENTY
DO YOU HEAR ME?

"Then they called on the name of Baal from morning till noon . . . At noon Elijah began to taunt them. 'Shout louder!' he said. 'Surely he is a god! Perhaps he is deep in thought, or busy, or traveling. Maybe he is sleeping and must be awakened.'"

— 1 Kings 18:26-27

"He who watches over you will not slumber" (Psalm 121:3). Our God, the only *true* God, never sleeps. He may be deep in thought, but we, his children, are always the subject of his thoughts, for he is mindful of us, and his thoughts toward us are precious and vast (Psalm 139:17). He may be constantly busy and hard at work, but our Lord is living to love us, watch over us, care for us, and intercede for us. Furthermore, although God does indeed "travel", he does not go off on vacation and leave us behind, but rather he always travels with us and goes before us, for it is written that "the LORD your God will be with you wherever you go" (Joshua 1:9). Who else and what else in this world can we trust to be as faithful and dependable as our unchanging God? Is there anyone else we can call upon at any time of day and in any place? Is there anyone who would respond to us with such perfect words of wisdom, peace, and indescribable comfort in every situation? There is no one like him. The Lord is our God, and what a privilege and gift it is that he is also our personal Savior and Abba Father.

Whatever idols we may set up for ourselves—an ideal, a person, a possession, an achievement—these do not, will not, and cannot satisfy our deepest needs and desires. We do not need to shout at God with eloquent, rehearsed, or refined speech, for he hears the quiet weeping of our souls, and before even a word is uttered on our feeble lips, he has heard our cry. There is no one else in this world who can understand our hurting and breaking hearts as completely and thoroughly as the Lord.

I am pleading and begging before the Lord today for his healing touch on my mind and my heart. Knowing that he is altogether loving, powerful, and sovereign over all things, I can fall trustingly into his open arms, deeply reassured that I will be tightly wrapped by my God's beautiful, glorious love that can quench every single longing in me. There truly is none like our God.

PRAYER

Dear Abba Father,

You are always mindful of me, and your thoughts toward me are precious and vast. No one in my life is as faithful and dependable as you. Only you truly understand my hurting and weeping heart, and only you can hear the quiet crying of my soul, even before a word is uttered. Help me today to destroy the idols in my life—the idols I have set up, the idols I worship, the idols I believe can help me. These idols include people who I see as "ideal," possessions that I cling to, and achievements I have attained and hope to attain. These idols do not, cannot, and will not satisfy the deepest needs of my heart. Help me today to destroy them. I beg you today to heal my suffering mind and body. In the name of the one who listens and hears, Jesus, amen.

MOVING FORWARD:

- List the things and people you are depending on more than Jesus Christ: doctors, counselors, medications, friends, books, money, your achievements, worldly philosophies, technology, etc. All of these things and people can be important as you manage your mental health problems, but none can be *more* important than Christ, your creator. If anything is more important than Christ, it has become your idol. Pledge today to put Christ first in the management of all your mental health problems. "Trust in the Lord with all your heart and do not lean on your own understanding. In all your ways acknowledge him, and he will direct your paths" (Proverbs 3:5-6, NKJV).

Who are you trusting the most for the treatment and healing of your mental health?

TWENTY-ONE
BUT I CAN'T HEAR YOU

"The LORD said, 'Go out and stand on the mountain in the presence of the LORD, for the LORD is about to pass by.' Then a great and powerful wind tore the mountains apart and shattered the rocks before the LORD, but the LORD was not in the wind. After the wind there was an earthquake, but the LORD was not in the earthquake. After the earthquake came a fire, but the LORD was not in the fire. And after the fire came a gentle whisper."

— 1 Kings 19:11-12

Have you ever noticed how even a very dim light can seem to shine wondrously brightly against a backdrop of complete darkness? Or how even the smallest murmur can seem to resonate surprisingly loudly in a quiet and still room? In contrast, wouldn't you logically conclude that a soft whisper would be left lost and undetected following the screech of a forceful wind, the heavy rumble of an earthquake, and the crackle of a blazing fire? Perhaps. Except if it is the whisper of God.

I don't know about you, but I likely wouldn't have

expected God to speak to Elijah with a gentle whisper. After orchestrating such a majestic prelude of tearing winds and flying rocks, I would have anticipated an even more dramatic climax of his passing presence. Yet he chose to catch us by surprise with the inconspicuous nature of a whisper, one that may seem insufficient and incapable of reflecting his all-surpassing glory. How puzzling this can be, yet at the same time, how appropriate. If you have ever conversed with people who have soft voices, you might remember having to strain your ears and pay extra close attention to their lips, eyes, and body gestures to properly understand the things they were trying to express. Perhaps the Lord wants us to seek him and watch for him with a vigilance and alertness analogous to this kind of focused attention. "Be still before the LORD and wait patiently for him" (Psalm 37:7), we're told. Yes, sometimes God may choose to *be* silent, but aren't there times when we miss his voice merely because his whisper is drowned out by the clanging and clanking of the chaos and distractions in our lives?

The Lord who quieted the winds and waves can still the stormy gales of our souls as well, leaving us ready and able to catch every single word that reaches down to us from him.

PRAYER

Dear great and majestic God,

You know and understand my mental, emotional, and physical deficiencies. Because of these struggles, I sometimes can't hear you as you respond to my prayers. The storms of my life seem to drown out some of your soft answers to me. When my anger erupts, you whisper, "I care for you"; when my life seems to be crumbling, you gently remind me, "I will never leave you or forsake you"; when I feel unclean, you say in a soft voice, "I love you". Please help me be still and wait patiently for you—your presence, your gentle answers, your encouragement, and when necessary, your reprimand and discipline. After every earthquake and fire in my life, I will wait patiently for your gentle whisper. In the mighty and gentle name of Jesus I pray, amen.

MOVING FORWARD:

- When you are waiting for God to answer you in a gentle whisper, open the Bible and read it. In most cases, he will speak to you gently through his written Word. Underline the special words he says to you, and even write down the request you have and, later, the date he answered you. When you read that portion of Scripture from now on, your special note and date will remind you of God's presence with you and of his faithfulness.

- You may also wish to spend some quiet time in nature (e.g., in the garden, by the waters), inviting God to speak to you through stillness in the beauty and majesty of his creation.

When did you last spend a moment in complete silence, asking God to speak to you? What can you do to eliminate distractions from your life so that you can hear more clearly from him?

TWENTY-TWO
I CAN'T GO ON

"Elijah was afraid and ran for his life. When he came to Beersheba in Judah, he left his servant there, while he himself went a day's journey into the wilderness. He came to a broom bush, sat down under it and prayed that he might die. 'I have had enough, LORD,' he said. 'Take my life.'"

— 1 Kings 19:3-4

How often have I prayed these exact same words to the Lord: "I have had enough—*more* than enough." He certainly sees the depths of my pain, so why doesn't he just remove me from this life, right now?

Isn't it ironic that the reason why Elijah fled in the first place was to save his life. He was afraid of being killed by the king, so he ran . . . *for his life*. Yet upon arriving in the desert, one of the first things he did was pray that he would die. What changed? Did his journey leave him feeling hopeless about ever being freed from this pursuit, so that he would rather be taken by the Lord than to be captured by his enemies? Or was he simply so overwhelmed with exhaustion that all he felt he had the strength left for was to lie down, sleep, and maybe die? Have you ever felt as Elijah did?

There are so many days when I simply do not and cannot see an end to these struggles. I think that if the Lord allows this suffering to continue for the rest of my life, then it would be better for me to die *now*. Then there are days when I am so weary of fighting that I simply want to give up; all I desire is to close my eyes and wake up in heaven. But all this has yet to happen. I wish for death, but he desires life for me.

The Lord refreshed and provided for Elijah. Might he not do the same for me? When one extra day seems impossible to endure, somehow the Lord always sustains me and brings that day to pass. I feel like I have had enough, but God doesn't seem to think I have. So perhaps my cry for him to take my life must take on new meaning. I need to truly surrender to him every part of my life. I need him to take my pain, my hurts, my weariness, my discouragement, and my suffering, and turn my life into one that glorifies and pleases him as it was created to do.

PRAYER

Dear Lord,

Because of my mental health problems, I sometimes feel like I would rather die than continue struggling and suffering. I feel like I cannot endure another day. As you refreshed and provided for Elijah, please do the same for me. When I am tired of struggling, please give me strength. When I feel like I want to die, please give me reasons to live. Please give me a passion for life and a passion to fulfill your will for me. May your Holy Spirit and your angels protect me from harming myself. Please take my pain, my hurts, my weariness, my discouragement, and my suffering and turn my life into one that glorifies and pleases you, as it was created to do. I pray in the name of Jesus, the giver of life, amen.

MOVING FORWARD:

- Replace the thought *Take my life* with *Take my life and use it for your glory.*
- Replace the thought *I want to die* with *I want to die to myself and live for you Lord.*

- Replace the thought *I give up* with *I give up on myself, but I will trust completely in you.*

How and where do you find comfort and reasons to live that are in accordance with what the Bible teaches?

TWENTY-THREE
SHIELDED FROM UNBELIEF

"[You], who through faith are shielded by God's power until the coming of the salvation that is ready to be revealed in the last time . . . Though you have not seen him, you love him; and even though you do not see him now, you believe in him and are filled with an inexpressible and glorious joy, for you are receiving the end result of your faith, the salvation of your souls."

— 1 Peter 1:5, 8-9

I am overwhelmed by the grace the Lord has poured into my life. Sometimes I really take for granted the faith he has given me. I mean, how irrational and impossible it is to love and possess such indescribable joy in the God we have not seen and cannot yet see? How easy should it be for us to be thrown into doubt and even question his existence? The line between unbelief and belief is really quite thin, yet the dramatic difference between the two is astounding. On our own, it would not take much for us to turn our backs on God and quit this walk of faith. But because of this gift of faith from God to us, we will be shielded by his power until we see our Lord Jesus Christ fully revealed. I am not even going to humbly pretend that I am capable of holding onto this faith *on my own.* My confidence is not in myself; it is in the Lord who is able to do all things possible *and* impossible.

As I was speaking with a friend who is claiming no desire to follow the Lord and has dangerously drifted from the faith, my heart was deeply grieved for her, but yet it overflowed with tremendous thankfulness at the same time. I may have been, and am, beaten, thrown about, and wounded by my struggles, but I haven't lost my faith. Yes, there are moments of doubt and even anger, but God has protected me from completely turning away from him. How can I help but be filled with incredible joy because of his love for me? I can't explain it, but I know that those who seek *will* find, and when we finally see the Lord before our eyes, wow—what a jubilant day that will be.

PRAYER

My dear Heavenly Father,

You have chosen me for salvation and given me faith despite my mental illness. During times of mental distress, it is easy for me to be thrown into doubt, and I know it would not take much to quit this walk of faith. Yet I am confident today that it is your gift of faith and your power in me that will shield me from turning away from you. I am not capable of holding on to this faith on my own. My confidence is in you, Lord. Although I have not seen you, I love you and believe in you. Please fill me with an inexpressible and glorious joy as I receive the goal of my faith, the salvation of my soul. In the faithful name of Jesus, I pray, amen.

MOVING FORWARD:

- Take a cup, mug, or glass, and with a permanent marker write the words *faith* and *joy* all over it. Drink from it daily, and let it remind you that it is God who fills you daily with faith and joy. As you drink from this cup, ask God to fill you with faith and joy, and thank him regularly for these special gifts.

What have you read in the Bible that fills you with the faith and joy only God can give?

TWENTY-FOUR
WHEN ALL HOPE SEEMS LOST

"Always be prepared to give an answer to everyone who asks you to give the reason for the hope that you have."

— 1 Peter 3:15

Someone once asked me in a somewhat confused manner about the hope I seem to possess in God and the trust I seem to have in his ultimate control and purposes. I think what remained unsaid was why I didn't act like I had such tremendous hope within me. She must have wondered how I supposedly had so much to anticipate and look forward to, and yet, I kept hurting myself and wishing I would die. How could I weep and cry like there was no hope for a future if I believed in a God of hope and a future? How could I keep declaring that I felt helpless when I also declared to know the greatest Lord of all who promises in his Word to help me?

I wonder about this too. I am confident about the

eternal future I will have in Christ, but I easily lose hope. Why can't I just bite my lip, close my eyes, and endure?

I don't know if I can satisfactorily reconcile this apparent contradiction between what I know and declare and what I often feel, but my answer is simply this: God has so deeply and firmly implanted the hope of Christ in me that it can't merely "go away". No matter how many times and how sincerely I claim hopelessness, genuine hopelessness simply cannot exist in me because *nothing can ever separate me from his love.* God is faithful to his promises. He is alive in me, and his promise to never abandon me still stands true and is actively at work within me.

Perhaps the Lord wants to remind me that my hope should not, and does not ever, depend on my circumstances. It always depends on him alone. It matters not whether my situations are easy or difficult, good or not-so-good, for I can neither hope nor rely on these, which quickly alter and change. There really should be no difference in my responses to either bliss or sorrow, for my unchanging Lord is still the provider of everything and ruler over all.

The load on my shoulders may vary in heaviness with the coming and going of life events, but the same hands that soothe my aching heart still belong to the God who has eternally saved me from my sins. So the reason for my hope? Jesus Christ—what more can be said?

PRAYER

Dear God,

I sometimes do things to hurt myself, and sometimes I wish I would die. However, as your adopted child, I am confident about my future because my hope is in Christ. Thank you for reminding me today that my hope should not, and does not, depend on my circumstances, but always on Jesus Christ alone. Thank you that it is Jesus who died for my sins; it is Jesus who is able to forgive me for my past, present, and future sins; it is Jesus who rose from the grave, defeated death, and gives me eternal life. Help me, Lord, not to hurt myself, and give me the God-given desire to live. Replace my feelings of hopelessness with remembrances of the sure hope I have in you. Thank you for life. It is truly a gift from you. Jesus, you are my hope, my life, and my love. I pray this in your healing name, amen.

MOVING FORWARD:

- Talk to someone you know who is suffering from any type of mental health problem, such as anxiety, depression, bipolar disorder, eating disorder, addictions, etc. Tell them they too can have hope in Christ for their present and the future.
- Learn how to share your faith and hope in Christ by reading the book *Living the Gospel*, by Dr. Peter Golin.
- Thank God that he can, and will, use you in the midst of your deep struggles to draw others to himself and find ultimate healing in Christ.

How has God used you as his instrument to reach other people for healing and salvation, even in the midst of your deep pain and struggles?

TWENTY-FIVE
WHY MUST I SUFFER?

"Dear friends, do not be surprised at the painful trial you are suffering, as though something strange were happening to you. But rejoice that you participate in the sufferings of Christ, so that you may be overjoyed when his glory is revealed."

— 1 Peter 4:12-13

I think there is little question as to whether or not I am suffering right now, but I have often wondered whether what I am going through counts as *sharing in the sufferings of Christ.* After all, I am not persecuted for professing my love for him, and I am rarely mocked for identifying myself as a follower of Christ. So does my suffering fall into a separate category?

John Piper once wrote, "In choosing to follow Christ in the way he directs, we choose all that this path includes under his sovereign providence. Thus, all suffering that comes in the path of obedience is suffering with Christ and for Christ—whether it is cancer or conflict. And it is 'chosen'—that is, we willingly take the path of obedience where the suffering befalls us, and we do not murmur against God."[3] I can confidently say that if I had the choice to decide whether or not I would like to experience the pain and trials I am presently suffering, I would confidently declare, "no thank you." But it just so happens that the Christ-pursuing path I *have* chosen to walk contains the very kinds of suffering I would have liked to avoid. This makes all the difference, doesn't it? Suffering for the sake of suffering versus suffering for the sake of Christ.

Saying yes to Christ must mean saying yes to suffering whatever trials he has ordained for us, for "Jesus said to his disciples, 'If anyone would come after me, he must deny himself and take up his cross and follow me'" (Matthew 16:24). How then should I respond? Rejoice. Rejoice that I have the privilege of sharing in his sufferings. Rejoice that when his glory is revealed, I will be absolutely and completely overjoyed.

Let me continue to obediently walk this narrow road, always confident that I am indeed on the right track, for this is the path leading me to my glorious home.

PRAYER

Dear Heavenly Father,

I am suffering great emotional pain right now, yet I have chosen to follow Christ under his sovereign providence. I am willing to take the path of obedience even when it leads to suffering, whether that suffering is because I identify myself as a Christian, or specifically due to my mental illness. Help me never to murmur against you. Teach me how to deny myself, take up my cross daily, and follow you. Teach me how to rejoice in every experience of suffering I have the privilege of sharing in Christ's suffering, and I know I will be completely overjoyed when his glory is revealed. Let me continue to obediently walk this narrow road. Help me be confident that this path is leading me to my glorious eternal home. I pray these things in the name of Jesus, the one who suffered for me, amen.

MOVING FORWARD:

- Read one of the following books on the topic of suffering; their words will surely encourage and bless you.

    - *Where is God When It Hurts* by Philip Yancey
    - *Walking with God through Pain and Suffering* by Timothy Keller
    - *Suffering in the Sovereignty of God* by John Piper and Justin Taylor
- Write down how the suffering you are experiencing has helped you learn more about the character of God and perhaps even strengthened your faith. Remind yourself that you can rejoice because the full glory of God will be revealed to you one day.

What suffering are you experiencing right now, and in what ways might God be calling you to be grateful for these trials?

TWENTY-SIX
GRACE FOR THE HUMBLE

"All of you, clothe yourselves with humility toward one another, because, 'God opposes the proud but gives grace to the humble.'"
— 1 Peter 5:5

I am good at turning people into my enemies in my heart and in my mind. If I meet a pretty girl, a thin girl, a smart girl, a girl who is liked by *my* friends, a girl who succeeds greatly, a girl who acts as if I am not worthy to be her friend, she has easily become an enemy of mine. Perhaps I feel threatened by her, or perhaps I am simply envious of all she represents. Whatever it is, if ever I see or think of her, I feel even more incapable, useless, and worthless than usual.

Why is this so? Do I, for whatever reason, think I should be "better" than others somehow? Am I unwittingly exalting myself above people, or do I simply have difficulties coming to terms with the reality that I'm really not as great as I might think? Rather than clothing myself with pride, I must choose to cover myself with humility. The position of the humble servant of the Lord is not "pitiful" or "shameful"; it is the most favorable of all, for upon the person who is humble, grace is lavishly poured out and abundantly given. It is God who endows us with desirable gifts, and it is he who exalts and humbles. What good is it for me to appear triumphant and victorious in my own eyes, when I so desperately rely on his grace that is most richly found in the place of humility? Jesus, who being in very nature God, willingly humbled himself to the nature of a servant in human likeness (Philippians 2:6-7). Can't I, a sinful human being much more deserving to be brought low, humble my own self before God and others, viewing myself in sober judgment, giving all praise to God and boasting in myself no more?

PRAYER

Dear loving Heavenly Father,

I want to clothe myself in humility, but my pride keeps showing up as a daily temptation. Not only are you unhappy with the proud, but you also oppose them. You promise to pour out your grace on those who show humility toward one another. Teach me how to clothe myself in humility toward all people, including my family and friends, and especially those who suffer from mental health problems. As I show humility, pour out your grace to me; when I am proud, gently guide me into humility, where grace may abound. Remind me that my worth is secure in you, and may I not attempt to push down others in order to exalt myself. Help me also to see other people in your church who suffer from mental illnesses as dear adopted children in your kingdom so that they may become treasured people in my life. Teach me how to honor them, respect them, and bless them. Please forgive me for any past attitudes of pride and disrespect. In the name of Jesus, the giver of grace to the humble, amen.

MOVING FORWARD:

- Meet with another Christian who suffers from

a mental disorder and ask them to share some of their daily struggles in life. Ask them how you can help them and pray with them. When you see them in church, sit with them, greet them warmly with Christian love, and encourage them. Remember to do all this with a humble heart as a servant of the Lord.

What other people do you know who have a mental illness? In what ways can you reach out to them with sincere love and kindness?

TWENTY-SEVEN
MY ANXIOUS HEART

"Cast all your anxiety on him because he cares for you."
— 1 Peter 5:7

God cares for me. I think I need to be *overwhelmed again* by this truth. God, who is infinitely more glorious, powerful, strong, and mighty than anything or anyone I can ever imagine, *cares* for measly little *me*? God cares for me, with all my sinfulness, ingratitude, stubbornness, and unwarranted pride? And he wants more? He wants my anxiety too?

God doesn't just care *about* me in a detached, passive way; he actively cares *for* me. He doesn't only care like I care about whether or not it will rain tomorrow. He cares for me as a parent cares for his child. He ensures that I am provided for, that I am well-protected, and that I have everything I need to thrive and flourish into who he has created me to be. God wants me to place my anxiety upon his shoulders because he knows that *my* shoulders would likely break under the heaviness of it all. He also desires to remove all my anxiety so that no trace of it would detract from the full joy and abundant life he wills for me.

We need not remain under the domination of anxiety any longer, for we weren't designed to live fretful lives plagued with endless concerns, worries, and trepidations. God is nudging us to break free from this bondage and cast our burdens and cares upon him. So will we do precisely this?

Lay it all down before our King, for he loves us and longs to carry the anxieties of his beloved children.

PRAYER

Dear caring God,

Thank you for not just caring about me, but for caring for me. Thank you for the food you provide, for my clothing, my housing, my safety, my education, and my work. Thank you for my salvation in Christ and my spiritual growth. Thank you for caring for my physical and mental health. Thank you for your everlasting love to me. You know and understand all my anxieties, and like a caring father, you desire to take these burdens from me. Please teach me how to cast my anxieties on you, lay my worries at your feet, let go of my burdens, and fully trust you to take care of every aspect of my life. Show me how to do this daily as you build my faith in Christ. Please forgive me when I fail. May your Holy Spirit and your Holy Scripture purify me and help me break free from the bondage of my anxiety. I pray this in the name of Jesus, the Prince of Peace, amen.

MOVING FORWARD:

- Memorize the following two Scriptures: 1 Peter 5:7 and Philippians 4:6-7.

- "Casting all your anxieties on him, because he cares for you" (1 Peter 5:7).
- "Do not be anxious about anything, but in every situation by prayer and petition with thanksgiving present your requests to God. And the peace of God, which transcends all understanding, will guard your hearts and your minds in Christ Jesus" (Philippians 4:6-7).

- When you notice yourself worrying or feeling anxious, physically open your hands and arms as an act of letting go of those worries and anxieties. With these same open hands and arms, receive the comfort and reassurance that comes only from your Heavenly Father.

Practically speaking, what does "casting all your anxieties on him" mean to you?

TWENTY-EIGHT
WHY DO YOU SEEM SILENT?

"So Eli told Samuel, 'Go and lie down, and if he calls you, say, "Speak, LORD, for your servant is listening."'"

— 1 Samuel 3:9

It is so frustrating when people are distracted in conversation and listen only half-heartedly to what you have to say. Their "mmm-hmm's" and "uh-huh's" never fall in the appropriate places, and it is clear that though their eyes appear to be fixed on yours, their attention is focused elsewhere. Their fidgety bodies make it plain that they cannot wait for you to finish talking so that they can concentrate on the perhaps more "important" thoughts currently dominating their minds.

I have to admit, I have often been such an "otherwise-occupied listener" myself. Rather than devoting my complete attention to the person I am conversing with, my mind is in several places at the same time. I am sorry to say I must have annoyed and exasperated many individuals because of this kind of distracted listening.

I wonder how this multi-tasking nature of our minds affects the ways we communicate with God. I wonder if we couldn't better hear what our Lord has to say to us if we would commit to him our full attention at all times. I wonder how many times we have failed to hear his voice for no other reason than because we have been distracted by other things.

The Lord is delighted when our thoughts and hearts are captured by him and tuned in to his voice. Wouldn't he be pleased if we would surrender all our thoughts to him, proclaiming to him with excitement and anticipation that we, his servants, are indeed listening? I wonder if his "silences" wouldn't ring with encouragement and wisdom if we would fix our eyes and ears on nothing but the Lord.

I don't need to wonder. I know it's true. God longs to speak life and direction into our emptiness and confusion, so let us affirm together that *yes Lord*, we are listening.

PRAYER

Dear Lord,

I confess to you that I can be a poor listener. I often cry out to you regarding my struggles and pain, but then I fail to give you my full attention in awaiting your response. I am so occupied with my own problems that sometimes I fail to see how you work through them and how you speak to me, your servant, through them. Here I am, Lord, today, surrendering my thoughts, my heart, and my full attention to you. Speak, Lord, for your servant is listening. Help me to listen, to hear, and to obey you—today, tomorrow, and every day. I pray this in the name of Jesus, my Great High Priest, amen.

MOVING FORWARD:

- After praying to God, open a Bible and ask Jesus to speak to you through his Word. Read a portion of the Scriptures with the understanding that the Holy Spirit is communicating to you by his wisdom, through that portion of his Word. Then, lie down or kneel, meditate on what you have read, and say to God, "Speak, Lord, for your servant is listening."

What are some ways you can increase the time you are spending truly listening to the Lord, with a heart and mind free from distraction, waiting before him in silence and anticipation?

TWENTY-NINE
HOW DO I LOOK?

"But the LORD said to Samuel, 'Do not consider his appearance or his height, for I have rejected him. The LORD does not look at the things man looks at. Man looks at the outward appearance, but the LORD looks at the heart.'"

— 1 Samuel 16:7

When will I finally learn to see as the Lord sees and look at the things he looks at? When will I finally learn to truly value the things the Lord values and hold dear to my heart those things he treasures?

In our culture today, the emphasis given to people's physical appearances very likely exceeds that which had been present at any other time. Yet if the Lord, who *formed* and *created* our outward appearances, doesn't worry about how we look, then why should we? Truly, why should an individual's physical appearance, which is extremely malleable and subject to sometimes radical change, have *any* bearing on how that person is viewed or treated?

I must admit that I see aspects of my own physical

appearance as much more significant than they really are. In particular, I cannot understand why I am so afraid of gaining weight. What exactly does gaining weight mean to me? Why does it feel like the end of the world if I gain even a tiny bit of weight?

I'm not sure I can answer any of these questions, but I do know that this intense fear of mine and other insecurities I face are unhealthy because they disregard the beautiful and creative work that God has revealed even in even imperfect beings. Yes, we are all flawed in some way or another, but we were also all created in the image of God. If I endlessly criticize and show disdain for aspects of myself and others, am I not insulting the work of my altogether lovely creator who is the most beautiful of all things?

And then what about my heart? I could choose to exert all my energy on improving my physical appearance, but at the end of the day, what is on the outside will waste away. It is the things inside our hearts that will be renewed (2 Corinthians 4:16). Why don't I work on developing those characteristics and traits that the Lord desires of me? They are what he looks at.

It truly is time for me to see the way God sees—looking not at the superficial, but rather on the beauty God has placed inside us all.

PRAYER

My dear Creator,

Thank you for creating me the way I am. Thank you for looking deep into my heart and seeing me the way I truly am. Help me to value in myself what you value when you look at me. I look at myself and usually don't like what I see as I compare myself to others (e.g. my weight, my height, my face, my hair, my figure, my skin blemishes, my scars, etc.). Help me to thank you regularly for the way you have made me physically. Give me the grace to accept what cannot be changed, and help me to change what needs to be changed and can be changed through a healthy lifestyle. I want to move my gaze past my body so that I can concentrate my efforts on my eternal soul within me. Change my heart, Lord, and make me more like Jesus. I am created in the image of God, so help me behave as Jesus, my God, would. This I pray in the name of Jesus, my creator, amen.

MOVING FORWARD:

- Make two lists of the qualities of Jesus you admire and love the most. On the first list, write down what you like about his character and his actions. For example: loving, kind, faithful, gentle, forgiving, patient, and sinless. On the other list, write down what you like about his physical appearance. For example: _____, _____, and _____. Notice there is nothing to put on this second list, nothing to admire in Jesus' physical appearance. As the Bible says about Jesus, "he had no form or majesty that we should look at him, and no beauty that we should desire him" (Isaiah 53:2, ESV). As you compare your two lists, remember that in the same way, your *character and actions* are what will attract others to Christ and help you fulfill his mission on this earth. Your physical attributes, while loved by God and need care through healthy living, are temporal. Focus your mind on matters of your soul. These are the things that will last for all eternity.

Have you ever wondered what Jesus physically looked like? Was his physical appearance important in any way for his work on earth?

THIRTY
FIGHTING FOR JOY

"I know that there is nothing better for men than to be happy and do good while they live."
— Ecclesiastes 3:12

I have been particularly teary these past weeks, such that every little thing is enough to trigger me to burst into sometimes unexplainable tears. I suppose I feel so overwhelmed by all the pain, disappointments, and stresses in my life that I have thoroughly depleted my coping resources for even my smallest daily stressors. I start crying when a driver cuts me off in traffic, when an acquaintance fails to return a friendly smile, and even at the thought of having to get myself out of bed to fulfill my most basic responsibilities for a given day. I ask myself: Why must I continue carrying this burden? Why must I continue fighting? Why must I continue *trying*? What is the *point* of it all?

It is then when I am reminded of these words in the book of Ecclesiastes: "I know that there is nothing better for men than to be happy and do good while they live" (3:12). And isn't this precisely what God desires for our lives? There is nothing better, for God is pleased and glorified when we discover that he is only true source of joy and happiness.

We need to strive to be happy and satisfied, for this is God's very gift to us (Ecclesiastes 3:13). Our situations and circumstances may not necessarily cause us to be happy, but we can accept them with joyous hearts because they have been prepared and purposed by God for our good. There is a time to weep and a time to laugh, a time to mourn and a time to dance (Ecclesiastes 3:4), yet regardless of what "time" it may be, there is nothing better for us than to do good and be glad. Let us not forget that the greatest joy we can experience comes from living in submission and faithful obedience to the will of God in every area of our lives. Without this goal to please God in all we do, everything truly is meaningless. "Now all has been heard; here is the conclusion of the matter: Fear God and keep his commandments, for this is the duty of all mankind" (Ecclesiastes 12:13).

PRAYER

Dear Lord,

I feel so overwhelmed by all of my pain, disappointments, and stresses in life. Although I believe in you, I don't always rely on your wisdom from the Bible to help me cope with my stressors and burdens. Please forgive me for neglecting to look to you for help. Is my only true source of joy and happiness in you? Are you truly glorified and pleased in my actions? Am I relying on you and your goals and principles for my life? If you are not pleased, forgive me. You are most pleased with me when I find all of my satisfaction in you. I accept my present circumstances not because they make me happy, but because they have been prepared and purposed by you, for my good. You will increase my joy as I live through my disappointments in full submission and faithful obedience to your will in every area of my life. I accept your Word today that there is nothing better for me than to be happy and do good for your glory. I pray these things in the name of Jesus, the one who brings me joy, amen.

MOVING FORWARD:

- Identify several things that make it difficult

for you to find joy and happiness in the Lord. These may include your symptoms of depression or anxiety or other mental health concerns.

- Search in the Bible for biblical truths that speak to these particular struggles. If you are not completely obedient to God's Word in these areas, write down the changes you need to make, and ask the Lord to help you make those changes in your thoughts, words, actions, and attitude.

Where do you look to find your joy and happiness? How can you seek these things in God so that you can please him and keep his commandments?

THIRTY-ONE
I KNOW BEST

"But the people refused to listen to Samuel. 'No!' they said. 'We want a king over us. Then we will be like all the other nations, with a king to lead us and to go out before us and fight our battles.' . . . The LORD answered, 'Listen to them and give them a king.'"

— 1 Samuel 8:19-20, 22

Just as the Israelites weren't satisfied with what the Lord had prepared for them, I am often dissatisfied with various circumstances in my life. I tell God that I want this, this, this, and that because *then* I will be just like everyone else, or *then* I will finally be victorious, or *then* I will no longer be confused about the direction in which my life is heading. The list goes on. And just as the Lord provided the Israelites with the king that they longed for, sometimes he grants me some of the things I ask for. But then, similar to the Israelites, whose subsequent kings frequently did not resemble the "perfect" king they'd hoped for, many times, what I'd thought would be solutions to my problems turn out otherwise. I am reminded again and again to seek the will of the Lord rather than the fulfillment of my desires.

The fact that God leads me, has gone before me, and fights for me casually slips my mind in times when I feel alone and without help in my struggles. I cry to God for immediate help or satisfaction, substituting the good that God is in fact already doing. As I experience the results of *my* requests, which God willingly grants me, I realize again and again that it is only in God and from him that I will ever receive the help and provision I truly need. I come back full circle again before the Lord with desperate pleas, but this time, I cry for more of him and his goodness—not for the fulfillment of futile longings that only leave me thirsting for more.

PRAYER

Dear God,

Because of my mental health struggles, I sometimes ask you for things that are not good for me—things that do not bring you glory. As my Heavenly Father, please provide me only with the provisions I truly need. May your will be done in my life rather than the fulfillment of my frequently selfish desires. Please help me to understand that you know my future, and you know what is best for me. Help me to trust you fully. Please go before me, as my Lord, and lead me. When I feel alone and am unable to think clearly due to anxiety, when I exercise poor judgment due to depression, and when I am unable to control my feelings and emotions, please be my King and fight my battles for me. When I am weak, you are strong. I pray these things in the strong name of Jesus, the Lord of lords, amen.

MOVING FORWARD:

- On a sheet of paper, make up two prayer lists. Label one list "What I Want," and the other list "What I Need." Bring them both to the Lord in prayer on a regular basis and ask him to answer your prayers according to his will. Check prayers off as God answers them, and see how God is not only faithful, but he is also full of mercy and grace.

How can you make sure that in your prayers, you balance supplication, or asking God for something earnestly, with prayers of adoration, confession of sins, and thanksgiving?

THIRTY-TWO
WORK IN PROGRESS

"In the beginning God created the heavens and the earth. Now the earth was formless and empty, darkness was over the surface of the deep, and the Spirit of God was hovering over the waters. And God said, 'Let there be light,' and there was light."

— Genesis 1:1-3

Someone once wrote that "since God freely created the universe by his Word, out of nothing, we can expect God to continue to act in that way."[4] Don't we depend and rely on God to continue creating wondrous things out of nothing? Who are we without God? No one. What are we without God? Nothing. What good can we accomplish without God? None. What victory can we gain without God? None. Oh, how we need him to create *something* in and through us!

When my heart feels faint, my strength thoroughly zapped, my spirit dry, and my mind completely worn, I can do nothing but wait for the Lord to renew my emptied self. On my own, I am helpless to restore this brokenness in me; I can only trust him to create again a pure heart and a faithful spirit that longs only for him. In the same way that he didn't create the world to be empty but rather to be inhabited by us (Isaiah 45:18), he didn't create our souls to be empty, but rather to have his Spirit reside in us (1 Corinthians 6:19).

It isn't that God simply *was* a creator; he *is still* our most perfect and beautiful creator. An artist continues to mold, shape, and add special touches to a piece of artwork until it is complete and he or she is satisfied. In the same way, "He who began a good work in you will carry it on to completion until the day of Christ Jesus" (Philippians 1:6). This is something we can hold on to: no matter how defeated or beaten we may feel, we know that this is not the end. God's creative work in us has not been completed yet. We know that the end result will be nothing less of glorious, for we are being transformed into his likeness day by day.

PRAYER

Dear God,

You created the heavens and the earth, and you created me. Just as you didn't create the world to be empty, but rather to be inhabited by people, you didn't create me to be empty, but rather to have your Spirit reside in me. You are the most perfect and beautiful creator. Thank you for the work you have done in me, and the work you will continue to do in me. No matter how defeated or beaten I sometimes feel, your Word teaches me that this is not the end. Your creative work in me has not been completed yet, and you promise that the end result will be nothing less than glorious, for I am being transformed into the likeness of Christ day by day. I will trust you and cling to this promise all the days of my life. I pray this in the name of Jesus, the creator of heaven, earth, and my body, the temple of the Holy Spirit, amen.

MOVING FORWARD:

- Draw a picture of yourself as best as you can. It can even be a stick figure. Write on the same picture all the ways in which the Lord is transforming and renewing your heart and character.

- Now, on the bottom of the picture, write out Philippians 1:6 and meditate on it:
    - "He who began a good work in you will carry it on to completion until the day of Jesus Christ."

God cannot complete the work in you unless he has begun a work in you. The work begins at the point of salvation. Have you given your heart, life, and body to Jesus through faith, repentance, and surrender to Christ? If not, consider doing this now. Is there someone you trust who you can talk to about salvation in Christ?

THIRTY-THREE JUST BE HAPPY WITH ME, PLEASE?

"We are not trying to please men but God, who tests our hearts."

— 1 Thessalonians 2:4

I absolutely hate it when people aren't perfectly happy with me. If I detect even a slight hint of disapproval or displeasure, I sometimes go to desperate lengths to try and make things right again. From all my failed attempts to satisfy and fulfill others' wants, I have (perhaps belatedly) concluded that people are difficult, if not impossible, to please. But really, do I actually believe that I have the power and ability to control people's degree of happiness and contentment with me?

Paul understood how futile it is to focus on obtaining approval from men rather than from God. For one, people do not fully know the motives of our hearts, and because we are often unable to accurately express our true thoughts and feelings through our words and actions, we frequently stand at great risk of being misunderstood. But God tests our hearts and knows both our vile and noble intentions; thus, our desires to please him will always be evaluated with sound and right judgment.

You know, if our lives are lived in obedience to the Lord and are pleasing to God, people cannot help but sense the beauty and love of Christ flowing from us. Although this may not always be welcomed with glad hearts, our greatest task is not to leave people happy with us, but rather it is to bring the gospel of Christ to all people. I really think that the secret to having people pleased with us is by living our lives to please God. It is true that the world, blinded by sin, may hate what they *think* Christians represent, believe, and teach, but all we can do is continue living as we are called to live and loving others as we are called to love. We who are in Christ Jesus are no longer under condemnation from God, and if we follow closely in his steps, living in obedience to him, then we stand with no valid condemnation from the people of this world either.

PRAYER

Dear God,

I have been living a life where I usually aim to please people and myself, rather than you. Please forgive me for this self-centered attitude. Help me to live an obedient life pleasing to you, by loving you with all of my heart, soul, mind, and strength. My trials often blind me from seeing that I have been created to glorify you, my creator, my Lord, my King. Test my heart and see my true motives. Show me where I need to repent. Help me to seek your approval rather than the approval of people, who like me, all have deficiencies of various kinds and all fall short of the glory of God. I want to please others by loving them the way you love me. In the name of Jesus, my best friend, amen.

MOVING FORWARD:

- Write down the ten main goals of your life. For example: to be physically healthy; to be free from mental illness; to be financially stable; to be married; to have a caring family; to have a stable job; to own a home; to travel the world; to graduate from college; to be happy, etc. Now write down ten of God's main priorities for your life, according to the Bible. For example: to glorify God; to become more like Jesus in thought, attitude, speech and action; to love God with all of your heart, soul, mind and strength; to love people as yourself; to share the good news of Jesus; to worship God; to fellowship with God, etc. Now compare your two lists and ask God to test your heart. According to your lists, from God's perspective, are you living to please yourself and other people, or God?

In learning to please God first in all of your thoughts and actions, how often are you looking to the Bible, versus other sources, for instruction?

THIRTY-FOUR
CAN I FORGIVE?

"So Abram said to Lot, 'Let's not have any quarreling between you and me, or between your herdsmen and mine, for we are brothers. Is not the whole land before you? Let's part company. If you go to the left, I'll go to the right; if you go to the right, I'll go to the left.'"

— Genesis 13:8-9

I often long for there to be real *peace* in my relationships. Not the "calm before the storm" kind of peace, but a true peace that remains and prevails despite conflicts and disagreements that arise. I will be the first to acknowledge the rather large role I often play in disturbing whatever peace there may be. It pains me deeply to be a reason for the many problems that are experienced in my relationships. In my mind, I do not even need to be the instigator of an argument, nor do I need to be physically present in an argument. Even a mere discussion that remotely involves me can spark blame, frustration, anger, and several other negative emotions and words. Moreover, to my shame, I rarely exert much effort to repair the damage I have done. I rarely attempt to restore the peace. Unwilling to yield or strive for reconciliation, I allow anger to fuel, resentment to build, and grudges to form.

But here Abraham demonstrated for us a great model of problem-solving between human beings. What he avoided was more than animosity and hostility; he also avoided the loss of lives, which may have resulted from battles between herdsmen over limited resources in the land. "Each of you should look not only to your own interests, but also to the interests of others" (Philippians 2:4). It is so difficult to let go of what I feel to be justified reasons for bitterness, but no matter how much of a "right" I feel I have to hold grudges and withhold forgiveness, I *must* still love and still forgive. Love is not about calculating who deserves what or who doesn't deserve what. After all, Jesus gave his *all* for undeserving me—am I not willing to give up these embittered parts of myself in order to maintain, preserve, and strengthen my relationships with others and so live in a pleasing way for my God?

PRAYER

Dear God,

Is there true peace in my family and relationships? Show me where there are conflicts, unresolved anger, hostility, and emotional wounds and pain. Convict me of my wrongdoings and my need to repent before my family, friends, and you. Teach me how to forgive and not hold grudges—how to nail my reasons for bitterness on the cross, which you teach me to take up daily as I follow you. Please heal the emotional wounds and pain I struggle with. Touch me today in a supernatural way with your Holy Spirit, and heal me from my mental health problems. Today I choose to forgive my parents, brothers, sisters, children, extended family members, and friends. I forgive all their wrongdoings to me and ask that you bless them in a very special way. Help me to love them, and show me how I can restore a loving relationship with each of them. I ask you for this miracle in the name of Jesus, the God who forgives and heals, amen.

MOVING FORWARD:

- Draw a big cross on paper.
- Write down the names of all the people in

your extended family and even friends somewhere on that cross.

- Next to their names, write down any offenses that continue to give you emotional pain.
- Pray over each offense, forgiving each individual for each offense.
- Under that cross, write the following words of Jesus: "Whoever wants to be my disciple must deny himself and take up his cross and follow me" (Matthew 16:24).

Are you willing to forgive all members of your family and all of your friends for every offense, which may help in healing in your body, mind, and spirit?

THIRTY-FIVE
EVEN THE DARKNESS CANNOT HIDE ME

"For those who sleep, sleep at night, and those who get drunk, get drunk at night. But since we belong to the day, let us be self-controlled, putting on faith and love as a breastplate, and the hope of salvation as a helmet."

— 1 Thessalonians 5:7-8

Darkness can be comforting in many ways. Under its cover we are "free" to do what we wish without anyone seeing. We can put off whatever "face" we strive to maintain when others are around. Perhaps this is why I often prefer to engage in more harmful behaviors at night. I realize I can then sleep the pain away without having to worry about reassembling myself to appear "normal" before people the rest of the day.

Oh, but I must throw off this affection for darkness! My Savior has beckoned me and called me into the light, and it is to the *day* that I now belong, not to the darkness. My life has been hidden within the God in whom there is no darkness, so no matter what time of day it is, I must continue to walk as a child of light. The deeds that belong to the darkness can seem so enticing and captivating, but may I not forget that I have the full armor of God protecting me, keeping me perfectly safe from the fervent attacks of the evil one. "Everyone who does evil hates the light, and will not come into the light for fear that his deeds will be exposed. But whoever lives by the truth comes into the light, so that it may be seen plainly that what he has done has been done through God" (John 3:20-21).

How dearly do I cherish and cling to these truths? This is the question we must all consider. Do we hate the light, or do we love our God so much that we hate darkness? It can be immensely difficult to flee the deeds of darkness, but we must never, ever quit persevering, for with the help and power of our unfailing Lord, we can truly be set free from all these chains of sin.

PRAYER

Dear Savior,

Please forgive me for my affection for darkness. I am often drawn to darkness in my mental illness as I look for an escape from my emotional pain and grief. As you call me to the light, I wish to be there. In that light, I see your beauty and your love, your mercy and your grace, your healing and your peace. Please give me the desire and the strength to walk to the light and in the light, following Jesus. Help me to hate the darkness and love the light. And as I walk in the light, please expose any harmful deeds so that I may repent and be cleansed by your Holy Spirit. Teach me how to always present my problems to you in an honest and humble way, rather than using them as an excuse for sinful behavior. Help me to never quit persevering. I pray this in the name of Jesus, the light of the world, amen.

MOVING FORWARD:

- Memorize John 3:20-21: "Everyone who does evil hates the light, and will not come into the light for fear that his deeds will be exposed.

But whoever lives by the truth comes into the light, so that it may be seen plainly that what he has done has been done through God" (John 3:20-21).

- On a small clean sticker or label, write the words, "Jesus is the light." Stick this sign onto the light switch in your room. Every time you turn your light on and off, the words "Jesus is the light" will remind you to walk in the light—i.e. *in Jesus*—following his example.

Is your depression drawing you to love the dark and hate the light? How would it feel to lay this burden at the feet of Jesus today? Are there ways you can do this?

THIRTY-SIX
THE STING OF DISCOURAGEMENT

"Therefore encourage one another and build each other up, just as in fact you are doing."

— 1 Thessalonians 5:11

It can be very painful, given my sensitivity surrounding issues of weight and appearances, to hear comments such as "*this* person is so thin," or "*that* person has lost so much weight." These words exacerbate my already intense feelings of anxiety and fear. Sometimes I just desire reassurance and encouragement, but the words I hear feel more discouraging and dispiriting.

I often find it much easier to encourage others than to encourage myself. It can be easier to have faith in the work that God can do in *other* people's lives and be confident for them, while holding much more doubt about my own situations. I find that I am often "surprised" by the grace of God and his many "special touches" in my life. Should I be? Why shouldn't

I expect God to work miracles and wonders in my life? I don't mean to suggest that I somehow *deserve* his grace, for I certainly do not, but he has promised me an abundant life filled with his goodness and mercy—do I not expect him to fulfill his promises? Perhaps it is this attitude of disbelief that hinders me from fully seeing God's encouragement and comfort in so many areas of my life.

We need to encourage each other and build each other up, for it can be so easy to fall into doubt regarding the sureness of God's loving and sovereign activity in our lives. I may at times not feel particularly encouraged myself, but God *will* provide me with all I need and more so that I can be equipped to touch others with the hope and assurance that comes only from him.

PRAYER

Dear God,

I have been discouraged by the way I look and feel. As I compare myself to others, I am often filled with greater feelings of fear and anxiety. There are also times when I get caught up in thinking that you care for others more than you care for me. I know this is false. Please forgive me. Lord, encourage me through your Word, by your Holy Spirit, and through fellow believers in Christ. Help me expect miracles and wonders in my own life. I do not deserve your goodness, but I strongly believe in your mercy and grace. I do believe in your promises, knowing they are not just for other Christians, but also for me. As you encourage me, please equip me to be able to encourage others with the hope and assurance that comes only through Christ.

I pray this in the name of Jesus, the God who encourages, amen.

MOVING FORWARD:

- As we encourage others, we ourselves are encouraged. Consider the following words you can use to encourage others.

- "Your kindness has meant a lot in my life."
- "You have been a wonderful example to me regarding generosity, forgiveness, patience, goodness, etc."
- "When you pray for me I am strongly encouraged."
- "Thank you for your sacrificial service at church. I have been blessed by it."
- "You truly are a beautiful person, inside and out. Thank you for being a good role model."
- "I know you have failed before, but with God's help, you can succeed."
- "I love you very much, and there is nothing that will stop me from loving you unconditionally."

When was the last time you encouraged someone? What can you do to encourage another person today, especially someone who suffers from mental health difficulties?

THIRTY-SEVEN
THIRSTY

"The grace of our Lord was poured out on me abundantly, along with the faith and love that are in Christ Jesus."

— 1 Timothy 1:14

I deeply treasure those moments when God's blessings seem to overflow. In times when I sense his abundant grace flooding my life, I almost feel like a thirsty puppy frantically trying to lap up every last drop of water pouring from an overfilled bucket. I am determined not to miss even a trickle of the refreshing liquid! It is in those times when I feel that my Lord truly is sufficient for me. It is then when I am confident of his provision and care. It is then when I begin to imagine that all just might be well one day . . .

If only those moments would last.

I bring to mind what Jesus once said: "Whoever drinks the water I give him will never thirst. Indeed, the water I give him will become in him a spring of water welling up to eternal life" (John 4:14). The Lord does not say that we will be satisfied only for a little while; he said we will *never* thirst. Yes, his grace continues to build and build and build, so much so that not only are our present needs abundantly provided for, but his water of life wells up to *eternal* life as well. In those all-too-frequent periods of perceived dryness and weariness, I can remember those glimpses of bountiful grace that alone truly reflect reality. "And God is able to bless you abundantly, so that in all things at all times, having all that you need, you will abound in every good work" (2 Corinthians 9:8). There is not a second when I don't have all and probably more than all I need. Christ came so that we can have *life* and that to the full. Seize and count on that promise, for "he who promised is faithful" (Hebrews 10:23).

PRAYER

Dear Heavenly Father,

You have made promises to all followers of Jesus, and that includes people who suffer from mental health struggles like I do. In the same way that the apostle Paul had grace, faith, and love poured on him abundantly, you also promise these things to all born-again believers. Teach me what it means to have an abundant life in Christ. Please make all grace abound in me so that in all things, at all times, having all that I need, I will abound in every good work. In my periods of dryness and weariness, help me to drink from you. You are the living water that can satisfy me forever—in this life while I suffer from various health difficulties and in eternal life in heaven, where there will be no more pain and suffering. Today, I promise to trust in you, for you are faithful to your promises. I pray this in the name of Jesus, the water of life, amen.

MOVING FORWARD:

- As you read the Bible and come across a promise of God, underline it in red. Once you come to believe that the promise is for all Christians, including those who suffer from physical and mental health problems, highlight it in yellow. Soon you will come to realize that God's promises were, and are, written for you also. Here are two examples of God's promises:

- "For God so loved the world, that he gave his one and only Son, that whoever believes in him shall not perish but have eternal life" (John 3:16).
- "And we know that for those who love God all things work together for good, for those who are called according to his purpose" (Romans 8:28).

What reminds you of God's promises on a regular basis, and how can you remind others of his promises?

THIRTY-EIGHT
WHERE ARE YOU, GOD?

"The LORD is with you when you are with him. If you seek him, he will be found by you."

— 2 Chronicles 15:2

Even when I feel like my spiritual walk is dry and weak, I must remember that the Word of God is still a sharp, active sword that can penetrate through the toughest and most reluctant of hearts. I cannot stop sharing with others his life-giving gospel or stop praying for people's salvation just because I feel lukewarm in my faith. The Lord's great power is still faithfully at work, despite how distant and far he may seem to be in our lives. We must fervently seek the Lord regardless of how much or little we "feel like" doing so, and if praying is the means by which we draw near, then we must pray and seek, knowing that he will come near and be found by us.

Haven't we all asked the question, *Where are you,*

God? Maybe we asked out of confusion, or maybe we asked out of frustration. Perhaps we asked out of anguish, or perhaps we asked out of desperation. But let's not simply stop there. We have taken that first step in our pursuit of a deeper and more intimate knowledge of our God, and we must continue striving and sometimes straining to that end. Don't you long for your relationship with our Savior to grow and mature and bloom and flourish? We must not ever tire or grow weary of seeking the Lord. I can only pray and pray for the Lord to fill me afresh with his Spirit and ignite in my heart a growing passion for him as I follow after him one step at a time.

PRAYER

Dear Heavenly Father,
Help me to seek you when I am strong and when I am weak, when I am feeling spiritually rich and when I am feeling spiritually dry; when my symptoms are well-managed and when they are not well-managed; when I feel like it and when I don't feel like it. Teach me how to seek you fervently and how to cry out earnestly in desperation to you. As you answer me, please penetrate deep into my heart, through my lukewarm faith. When I cry out in my confusion or my frustration, "Where are you, God?" please answer me in a way that will leave me no doubt that you are with me, loving me, guiding me, caring for me, and healing me. Fill me afresh with your Spirit and ignite in my heart a growing passion for a deeper love relationship with you. I pray this in the healing name of Jesus, my heavenly physician, amen.

MOVING FORWARD:

- Get yourself a plant and begin caring for it. Remind yourself that regardless of how you feel, the plant requires regular care, such as watering and fertilizing. In the same way, God continues to care for you regardless of how you feel physically, emotionally, and spiritually each day. Remember that God cares for your plant by providing water, sunlight, and life. Just as your plant never stops longing for water and sunlight, remind yourself to never grow weary longing for Jesus, your spiritual water and light.

How have you found and experienced God as you pray and read his Word?

THIRTY-NINE
GOD, I DON'T KNOW WHAT TO DO

"We have no power to face this vast army that is attacking us. We do not know what to do, but our eyes are upon you."
— 2 Chronicles 20:12

Sometimes I sense that God just needs to break my heart, stripping away all the comforts and securities I have grown accustomed to, so that I would find myself having nowhere else to turn but to the Lord himself. As painful as it may feel to be completely helpless and have no resources left in me to continue fighting, I suspect there is no better place to experience afresh the grace of God than here. As I recognize more and more my utter dependence on him in every tiny detail of my life, he allows me to see that without him, I am and have nothing.

As I think about all the ways in which God has strengthened me and granted me success in the past, I marvel at his pure grace in all aspects of my life. I had nothing of my own then, and I have nothing of my own now. Nothing has changed. God had blessed me then, and he blesses me now. He loved me then, and he loves me now. He knew my pain then, and he knows my pain now. These things haven't changed. Most importantly, *he* has not changed. He was faithful then, and he is faithful now. I feel this great army of doubt and fear attacking every vulnerable corner of my soul, and all I can say to the Lord is that I truly do not know what else to do. I simply pray that he would give me eyes of faith that can see him with perfect clarity, for I have no power to face this war. I can only look to God with anticipation and trust, believing that he will conquer, and he will win.

PRAYER

Dear Lord,

Please show me what comforts and securities I cling to that cause me to take my eyes off of you. Is it my family and friends, my education and job, my pride or my longing for earthly pleasures? Because of my present mental and emotional state, I do find myself at this time completely helpless, and have no resources left in me to continue fighting. Fill me with a special measure of your grace today. As I learn to depend on you more and more, pour your grace and blessings on me. I feel a great army of doubt and fear attacking every corner of my soul. Please give me eyes of faith to see you with perfect clarity, believing and trusting that you will conquer and win for me. You have blessed me before, during, and after my bouts of depression and anxiety. You have always been faithful to me, and I thank you. I love you dearly. I pray these things in the powerful name of Jesus, amen.

MOVING FORWARD:

- Make a list of the "good things" in your life that have occurred in the past or could occur in the future, which may cause you to take your eyes off Jesus and place your dependence on "them." Examples could include money, a secure job, excellent health, good looks, a prideful attitude, and special connections we have with people. If you depend on them more than Jesus, they have become your idols and your gods. Sincerely ask God to remove them from your life if ever they were to draw you away from trusting Jesus.

Are you aware of the spiritual forces that are attacking you on a daily basis? How can you remind yourself that every victory has been won in Jesus?

FORTY
LOSING THIS BATTLE?

"For the battle is not yours, but God's."
— 2 Chronicles 20:15

Due to my rather dreadful sense of direction, I have become very reliant on Google Maps to help me find my way to places I have never been before. When I have absolutely no clue as to which direction to head or what routes to take, the maps provide me with just the right information and guidance I need. When they tell me to turn right, I turn right. When they tell me to go straight for 5.72 miles, I do (approximately) just that. And what do you know? I arrive safely at my destination!

Right now, in this seemingly never-ending battle with sin, I want to be told exactly what to do and have the power to do exactly that. As an appointed soldier in this raging war against sin, I wish I could always clearly hear the Lord telling me where I should turn and what I must do. How I must be careful to not start taking matters into my own hands by attempting to devise my own strategies to conquer the Enemy! Let me not forget that even though I may feel caught and trapped in the middle of all the action and dangerous attacks, the battle is ultimately the Lord's. Even more, the outcome has already been determined. God's victory is assured, and hence, our victory has been secured.

The pull of sin and death seems to have such a strong grip on my life, but the power of our risen Lord has, in fact, broken all those chains away, leaving me free to enjoy the victory he has obtained. "For everyone born of God overcomes the world. This is the victory that has overcome the world, even our faith. Who is it that overcomes the world? Only he who believes that Jesus is the Son of God" (1 John 5:4-5). I cannot thank the Lord enough for giving me the faith to believe in his powerful name, for writing my name in his book of life, and for granting me the stunning privilege and honor to spend all of eternity in his very presence. When overwhelmed by the frequency and magnitude of my failures, I can't help but feel as if I'm fighting a losing battle. But let me remember that the war waged over my eternal destiny has already been won. All I can do in the meantime is continue to earnestly seek him and love him with everything I am, obeying him and trusting that he will soon bring me safely into his heavenly home.

PRAYER

Dear God,

Thank you that the work needed to be done for my salvation has been completed by you; that the outcome over sin and death has been determined by you; that by dying on the cross and rising from the dead, you have secured victory over my sin and my death. As I fight sin I am not fighting a losing battle, but a battle in which I cannot lose. My pain and trials cannot and will not stop me from achieving my victory with Christ. To achieve victory I must follow your direction in life and death, in faith and total surrender to your commandments. Help me not to devise my own strategies to overcome sin. May your Holy Spirit guide me to your roadmap, the Bible, as I look for direction to overcome every temptation and sin. I pray these things in the victorious name of Jesus, amen.

MOVING FORWARD:

- Make a new cover for your Bible or paste a new title on your Bible. Call it "Road Map to Victorious Living." Reflect on ways that God has guided you step by step in the past and how he is directing your paths today.

How many spiritual wars are you fighting with your own wisdom and strength, and how many are you fighting with your leader and partner in spiritual warfare, the Holy Spirit?

FORTY-ONE
THROUGH YOUR COMFORT

"Praise be to the God and Father of our Lord Jesus Christ, the Father of compassion and the God of all comfort, who comforts us in all our troubles, so that we can comfort those in any trouble with the comfort we ourselves have received from God."

— 2 Corinthians 1:3-4

I often find that God has quite a sense of humor. So many times when I feel defeated, my spirit is downcast, and I long to be comforted and encouraged, God sends people my way who are hurting and suffering, needing the relief I so desperately seek. At a time when I feel so incapable of offering any kind of consolation, I am led to people who need a loving touch. Doesn't that seem so ironic? If I am unable to comfort even myself, how could I possibly bring any comfort to other people?

I supposed it might have slipped my mind that the comfort my friends, family, and I need is that which comes only from God. It is he who relieves, he who eases, and he who heals. I sense that the Lord has given me a heart for the disheartened and the hurting, but might I realize that we are always merely the *conduit* through which *God's* comfort flows to lift up burdened and suffering individuals? It is not by our own intellects and skills that people's aching hearts are soothed; it is always by the power of God that any of us are healed.

Maybe I feel as if I am still awaiting his comfort to alleviate all this pain, but I can be assured that it *will* come if it hasn't already. After all, there are people around me to be comforted! If for no reason other than this, he will surely fill me with his comfort so that I can encourage others and point them to the source of *all* comfort.

PRAYER

Dear Heavenly Father,

You are the Father of compassion and the God of all comfort, who comforts me in all my troubles. In my mental health struggles I often feel alone; I feel like nobody understands me or cares about how I suffer every day. Thank you for reminding me that you can and will comfort me in all my troubles. Please comfort me even now, with the peace of God that surpasses all human understanding. Lord, I desperately need your comfort now and every day. And as you comfort me, help me to see the needs of people around me. Help me understand that all people experience physical and emotional pain, and all of us need to be comforted by you. Please use me as a conduit to comfort those whom you place in my path, even when I feel incapable of doing so. Help me realize that they are my neighbors whom I need to love as myself, and please provide me with the strength and wisdom I need to comfort them as you have comforted me. I pray this in the name of Jesus, the comforter, amen.

MOVING FORWARD:

- Ask God to place on your mind one person

right now who may need comforting. Pray for them right now, and then call them or email them. Spend a few minutes comforting them by encouraging them, blessing them, praying with them, crying with them, laughing with them, and being a good friend. As you do this, you yourself will be blessed and comforted by your Heavenly Father.

One of the names given to the Holy Spirit is the Comforter. What image does that bring to your mind?

FORTY-TWO
YOUR OVERFLOW IN MY SUFFERING

"For just as the sufferings of Christ flow over to us, so also through Christ our comfort overflows."

— 2 Corinthians 1:5 (BSB)

Going through my struggles has truly allowed me to see with deep compassion the suffering of those around me. Although the burdens we each bear are unique and perhaps tailored by God, I am able to say with greater conviction to those individuals, "I feel your pain." I may not fully understand the depths or degrees of their suffering, but when it comes down to it all, pain is pain, and I *can* understand how it hurts. Not only am I better equipped to empathize with their grief, but I can also offer to them the comfort that God graciously provides me. The comfort I receive is sometimes sporadic windows of peace amidst long stretches of chaos. It is sometimes moments of joy breaking out of periods of fear and desperation. Or sometimes it is sparks of renewed hope bursting out of my empty heart. Whatever form God's comfort may take, it strengthens, restores, and encourages the faith of all who receive it.

God's comfort does more than refill what has been swallowed by suffering; it *overflows* in God as well as in our lives. God so abundantly showers us with grace that in comparison, the comfort we receive can overshadow our present suffering. This is not to undermine the immense anguish and distress we experience, but rather, it gives us complete confidence that God's hand is at work in every situation and reminds us that his ultimate purpose behind our every struggle is always good.

PRAYER

Dear God,

I thank you that because of your suffering, you truly understand my suffering due to depression, anxiety, and harmful behavior. I also thank you that I am able to see the suffering of those around me because of my own suffering. Help me to feel with deep compassion the grief and pain of those people you have placed in my church, my family, and my circle of friends. Forgive me for often focusing only on myself and neglecting to see the needs of the people I love. As you comfort me, please give me the confidence that your hand is at work in every situation and remind me daily that your ultimate purpose behind my every struggle is always good. This I pray in the name of Jesus, the Prince of Peace, amen.

MOVING FORWARD:

- Memorize 2 Corinthians 1:5: "For just as the sufferings of Christ flow over to us lives, so also through Christ our comfort overflows" (BSB).
- Now underline the phrases, "sufferings of

Christ flow over into our lives" and "through Christ our comfort overflows" in your Bible.

- Highlight the words "our lives" and "overflows".
- Place a cup in a sink and pour water into it. Keep pouring until the cup overflows. As you do this, remind yourself of the stream of God's comfort and love that overflows in our lives, which never, ever ceases.

How do you understand the word "overflows"?

FORTY-THREE
STILL UNSURE

"For no matter how many promises God has made, they are 'Yes' in Christ. And so through him the 'Amen' is spoken by us to the glory of God."

— 2 Corinthians 1:20

Whatever the Lord has promised, that he will do. "Because God wanted to make the unchanging nature of his purpose very clear to the heirs of what was promised, he confirmed it with an oath" (Hebrews 6:17). Through Jesus, our forever priest who lives always to intercede for us, we have full assurance that what God has promised will be fulfilled. He has come to remove the guilt of our sins that had once barricaded our way to the Father, and he has become *the* way into the grace and forgiveness of God. Christ's blood has cleansed us from all our unrighteousness, so we now have the guarantee of the eternal inheritance God has promised to us.

My life often seems so unpredictable and unstable that even when I am graced by better moments, I still sit in tension and apprehension, anticipating the instant when my world will come crashing down once again. Even as I pray for today to be the start of a future free from these hard times, I cannot help but wonder how long into the day I will last before succumbing to one temptation or another again. But despite these uncertainties and the anxieties that come along with them, my hope in Christ is still that firm and secure anchor for my soul. When I begin to doubt God's ability to remember all the promises he has given or his power to bring them all to fulfillment, I must remember that he who promised is faithful and what he has promised is true. I must hold unswervingly to this beautiful hope, proclaiming my "amen" with complete confidence. I must trust that because of Jesus, the mediator of this new and glorious covenant, God has affirmed his promises not with maybes and perhapses, but with a victorious and triumphant *yes.*

PRAYER

Dear Heavenly Father,

I often break my promises, but you never do. Because of my mental health problems, I am sometimes unreliable and unfaithful to you and others. Please forgive me. I often doubt your promises, thinking they must be for other people, for "healthy" people. Why would I deserve to be blessed by your loving care? Today you have reminded me that it is not because of who I am but who Christ is that allows me to see your promises fulfilled in my life. In Christ, I have the promises of God's love, forgiveness of my sins, the care of my loving Heavenly Father, the comforting friendship of the Holy Spirit, and the gift of eternal life. Today I receive your promises as gifts I don't deserve. Thank you for your special promises to me. I pray these things in the name of Jesus, my faithful God, amen.

MOVING FORWARD:

- Write down three promises of God that are found in the Bible. You may consider putting these promises in a special box you can look back at any time.

- If you don't know where to begin, consider the following resources:
    - Go to your local Christian bookstore and ask for a book on God's promises.
    - Look in your study Bible.
    - Search the Internet.
    - Ask a pastor at your church.
- Now add a new promise of God each week, and claim them as truth. Read these promises regularly, especially when symptoms of your mental illness worsen. Pray and ask God to help you apply them in your daily life.

What promises in Scripture do you feel God fulfilling in your life now?

FORTY-FOUR
GRIEVING LOSSES

"So Esau despised his birthright."

— Genesis 25:34

How do we respond when we lose the things we once owned and possessed? I suppose we could try to retrieve or recover what we'd lost with all our might, we could convince ourselves that we really didn't like it "that much" in the first place, or we could decide that we really dislike the person who has what we *wish* we still had. And that's exactly what Esau did, isn't it? He despised the birthright he had sold to his brother on impulse, he developed a heart of hatred and jealousy toward his brother, and he desperately pleaded for his father to somehow grant him a blessing as well.

There are many things in my life that I regret losing—things I long to still have. Perhaps they have been lost because of fears and mistakes on my part, or perhaps I feel like they have been taken away from me "by force." I have come to realize that by deciding what I had loved isn't worth loving or what I had cared deeply about isn't worth my attention, I am, in fact, being dishonest to myself and dishonest before God. How can I, by *denying my pain*, bring my grief to the Lord in complete openness and truthfulness? The Lord doesn't need a filtered or edited version of my story. I believe my God of truth desires for me to lay every burden at his feet in total frankness and honesty. No matter how much I may have lost, let me remember this: "And my God will meet all your needs according to the riches of his glory in Christ Jesus" (Philippians 4:19). God will never leave me lacking. No, this is too much of an understatement. *My God will pour out his blessings into my cup until it overflows, and even then, he will keep on pouring*. That abundance is more accurate, and more importantly, it is a better description of our most gracious and *giving* Heavenly Father.

PRAYER

Dear God,

There are some things I have lost in my past that has caused great pain for me. These things include aspects of my mental and physical health, friends, family members, validation and affection from others, opportunities to serve you by serving people, and opportunities to grow in Christ-like character. Today, as I remember them, I grieve, and as I grieve, I lay that emotional pain at your feet. Please heal me from that pain, and restore joy to my life. Fill me with peace as you remind me of what I have not lost—the forgiveness of my sins, a regenerated heart, the gifts of your Holy Spirit and eternal life, your eternal love, and your promise of meeting all of my needs according to your glorious riches in Christ Jesus. I ask that you pour out your blessings into my cup until it overflows, and then, keep on pouring. This I pray in the name of Jesus, the provider of all my needs, amen.

MOVING FORWARD:

- Write down three to five things you have lost or given up that were very dear to you and that you deeply regret.

- Now lay them at the feet of Jesus in prayer, asking him to heal you from the emotional pain of their loss. Give up the burden of those losses forever. You may need to pray for this daily for the next few weeks.
- Write down three to five blessings you have recently received from God, and ask him to multiply them according to his glorious riches in Christ Jesus. Now look forward to receiving them from the Lord, and don't forget to thank him when they come.

What have you lost in your life that has resulted in great pain? If you have lost your first love for the Lord, are you willing to let the Lord restore this love in you and give you great joy? Why or why not?

FORTY-FIVE
MUST I GO ON?

"We were under great pressure, far beyond our ability to endure, so that we despaired and life itself. we felt we had received the sentence of death . . . But this happened that we might not rely on ourselves but on God, who raises the dead."

— 2 Corinthians 1:8-9

Oh, yes. Despairing of life. I am far too familiar with this. I ask myself how I can be so ungrateful and unappreciative of this precious *gift* of life that God has created, but I don't know how to answer myself, for I cannot bear to even think about, let alone *explain* all the reasons why I'm in pain. The hurt truly is so great that I am simply overwhelmed—overwhelmed to the point of desiring not only for my suffering to end, but for my life to end as well. What would having the sentence of death feel like? I imagine there would be little hope for escape, deliverance, or freedom, accompanied by constant feelings of denial and disbelief. Sounds familiar indeed.

"But this happened that we might not rely on

ourselves but on God, who raises the dead" (2 Corinthians 1:9). If we think about the immense hardships that Paul did not think he could endure, is it not astonishing how he was able to recognize the sovereignty of our *purposeful* God through it all? He knew their suffering was not merely a result of the cruel actions and sins of powerful men, but rather, they were in great pain so that they would learn to rely completely and fully on God. Can I not do the same? It has never been clearer to me that reliance on myself leads me further and further away from where I *need* to be—the place of total surrender to the Lord. God, who can raise the dead and bring an end to all hopelessness and despair, can surely give me that extra bit of strength I need to endure. Just fall on him. Just lean completely on him and trust that in doing so, I will be equipped with greater strength and ability than I can ever imagine possible.

PRAYER

Dear God,

During particularly difficult periods in my mental health condition, I often feel that I am under great pressure, far beyond my ability to endure, so that I despair even of life. I sometimes think my problems will kill me, and sometimes I think of suicide. Thank you for helping me get through these tremendously difficult times. Without your help, I would never have been able to endure. I understand that these things have happened as part of your sovereign plan so that I might not rely on myself but on you who raise the dead. Teach me how to totally surrender to you, especially when I am under great pressure and am even feeling suicidal. When I feel the sentence of death, strengthen me, save me, heal me, and equip me to continue following you. I pray this in the wonderful name of Jesus, the Good Shepherd, amen.

MOVING FORWARD:

- Suicidal thoughts can come to anybody, but they are more common to those suffering from mental health problems. It is good to be prepared with a plan of action to be able to stand firm when tempted. Consider the following plan of action:

1. Tell someone you trust. This could be a friend, pastor, youth leader, family member, therapist or mental health clinician, or your doctor.
2. Pray with that person for godly wisdom and courage to trust Jesus rather than your own feelings.
3. Do not be left alone if your suicidal thoughts and feelings remain. If necessary, go to the hospital emergency room, your doctor, or mental health care clinic. Contact your local or national crisis or suicide hotline and share your struggles with caring and compassionate individuals.

- Make a promise to God right now that you will never act on those thoughts of suicide because you love Jesus more than life and death. Even if you are struggling to believe in the good and sure promises of God, commit to trusting in his faithfulness. Be assured that having suicidal thoughts does not mean you need to act on them. These thoughts will pass, and God can and will replace them with life-giving ones.

Do you consider suicide as an escape from pain and suffering? In what ways is suicide absolutely contrary to his plan and purpose for you (e.g., building your character, bringing you healing, preparing you for eternal joy and wholeness with him)? What will you commit to doing today that will keep you safe and keep you from acting on suicidal thoughts?

FORTY-SIX
MY SPIRALING THOUGHTS

"And we take captive every thought to make it obedient to Christ."
— 2 Corinthians 10:5

"Finally, brothers, whatever is true, whatever is noble, whatever is right, whatever is pure, whatever is lovely, whatever is admirable—if anything is excellent or praiseworthy—think about such things" (Philippians 4:8). Sadly, many of the thoughts I harbor in my mind are hardly excellent or praiseworthy. How often do I dwell on thoughts that do not conform to the ways of Christ, let alone please him? I permit harmful and deceptive thoughts to enter, linger, and twist and twirl in my mind, allowing them to overpower whatever competing *God-honoring* thoughts there are. I have found that many of these thoughts do not just spontaneously emerge out of nowhere; they may be triggered by events that leave me overwhelmed and helpless, or they may result from smaller and more benign contemplations that slowly escalate and intensify. However they arise, I must still take captive *every* thought, both big and small.

I don't think the encouragement to focus our thoughts on wholesome things only means that we take all our negative thoughts and turn them into good. Rather, *from the start* we must strive to allow *only* those thoughts consistent with the wonderful truths of God to be matters we consider and dwell upon. If you imagine our minds to only be capable of holding a finite amount of information, it makes perfect sense that filling our minds with only the thoughts of Christ would naturally eliminate many harmful ones. As another example, just as how *stopping* negative habits and behaviors is often much more difficult than *replacing* them with positive ones, rather than attempting to rationalize or attempt to dispute unholy thoughts, it may be more efficient and practical to not concentrate on them in the first place. And honestly, although those destructive thoughts may seem pleasant to dwell on, ones that are obedient to the Lord and are honorable and holy produce true peace and joy that surpass anything we can dream of.

PRAYER

Dear Lord,

I frequently allow many harmful and unclean thoughts to enter my mind. I often dwell on them and allow them to control my emotions, especially when I am anxious and depressed. They are sometimes triggered by anger and frustration as I deal with my mental illness. Please teach me how to take captive every harmful thought, big and small. I know that negative thoughts will enter my mind, and I need your Holy Spirit to help free me from those thoughts before they bring me harm. Help me to quickly repent when I fail, and help me change my sinful habits and behavior. Please help me fill my mind with thoughts that are pure, lovely, admirable, excellent, and praiseworthy. I pray this in the cleansing name of Jesus, the healer of my body and spirit, amen.

MOVING FORWARD:

- Memorize the following phrases: "Turn Off" then "Turn On."
- When unclean thoughts enter your mind, say

the phrases "turn off'" then "turn on." Then begin to pray to the Lord to turn off your harmful thoughts and turn on his life-giving thoughts. Practice this regularly.

When was a time that you saturated your mind with the Word of God in order replace the harmful and unclean thoughts that had filled your mind? What was that experience like?

FORTY-SEVEN
PAIN I CANNOT BEAR

"To keep me from becoming conceited because of these surpassingly great revelations, there was given me a thorn in my flesh, a messenger of Satan, to torment me."

— 2 Corinthians 12:7

Although I may not be able to identify with Paul's "surpassingly great revelations," I think I can understand the feeling of having a thorn in my flesh—this sometimes dull, sometimes searing pain I cannot put from my mind for more than a brief while. Morning after morning, I wake up with this sense of overwhelming emptiness and dread. As I open my eyes to a new day, I am reminded of how incredibly alone and unloved I feel in this world and how much I desire to hide in the refuge of sleep to protect myself from feeling this tremendous pain. Yet even in my sleep, I dream of situations in which I am abandoned, lonely, neglected, and uncared for. There is no escaping this "thorn," for the sting it causes seems to have permeated through to every aspect of my being. Why is God doing this? Why is he not removing this pain from me? Is he keeping it there to prevent me from forgetting him? Is he keeping it there to remind me of my ultimate need for him and not myself? I get it, God. I get it. Can you please give me relief from this *now*?

All this pain is often overwhelming and seems totally unbearable, but the God who can easily release this thorn from me is choosing to allow it to remain as tightly wedged as ever before. There may be a million reasons why, but for me, it may just be a not-so-gentle reminder that I am completely and utterly dependent on the Lord to sustain me. Not by my power. Not by my might. But by his Spirit alone (Zechariah 4:6).

PRAYER

Dear Lord,

You have allowed my mental illness to be a thorn in my flesh. I don't know if it is from you or Satan, or whether it is given to strengthen me or to torment me. What I do know is that you are responsible for my sanctification and that because I love you and because I am called according to your purpose, all things work together for good. I believe in you and trust you, and I accept this thorn as your sovereign will for my life. May it always be a reminder that I am completely dependent on you to sustain me. I will continue to serve you, not by my power, not by my might, but by your Spirit alone. Dear Heavenly Father, I do pray, however, that you please give me relief from this thorn. Please heal me according to your loving kindness and according to your will. In the name of Jesus, who is sovereign over all, amen.

MOVING FORWARD:

- Write down the mental health problems you have, and next to that, write down some of the possible biblical reasons God would allow you to have such a thorn in your flesh. Here is an example:

Depression

- *To keep me from being proud and to help me rely on God's strength.*
- *To help me experience God's faithful comfort and security, which I cannot find elsewhere.*
- *To build in me Christ-like character.*
- *To help me take my eyes off the riches of this temporary world and concentrate on the heavenly.*
- *To equip me to help others suffering from similar mental health problems.*
- *To keep me grounded in the Scriptures and prayer.*

Where does your mental illness cause you to look more eagerly: deeper into this temporary present sinful world or to your permanent glorious home in heaven?

FORTY-EIGHT
GREATER THAN MY WEAKNESS

"But he said to me, 'My grace is sufficient for you, for my power is made perfect in weakness.' Therefore I will boast all the more gladly about my weaknesses, so that Christ's power may rest on me."

— 2 Corinthians 12:9

I have often wondered what "sufficient" actually means in this verse. Does it mean that his grace is *enough*? That his grace is *all I need*? As in, I wouldn't need to search for or long for more of anything because his grace is able to overpower every single one of my weaknesses and fill up every lack? His grace is sufficient, but I certainly haven't had enough of it. For each moment, I rely on his grace to provide me with a new breath to take. With each minute that passes, I trust that by his grace he will help me get through and endure another painful hour. Daily, I depend on his grace to face whatever challenges that come and to offer forgiveness and mercy to those who hurt and harm me. I need his grace to sustain me when everyone else seems to have abandoned me, and I need for his grace to heal me when to the world I am "broken beyond repair."

With God, there is absolutely no reason for me to try to conceal my weaknesses. I truly do desire to see the power of God clearly and gloriously displayed, and if by my becoming less, the greatness of God is magnified, then I have all the more reason to gladly boast about my weaknesses! I long for all the world to be able to *see* and personally experience the awesome power of our God, so maybe it is time for me to be more willing to tear down the towers of pride I've been building in my life. Maybe it is time to start viewing my weaknesses as avenues through which God's grace and power can flow rather than as faults I need to deny and hide. And really, no matter how empty we may become, his grace and power will always be sufficient to fill us up and overflow in our lives, helping us and protecting us in our every hour of need.

PRAYER

Dear Heavenly Father,

Forgive me for hiding my weaknesses. I am ashamed of my mental health issues, for to me they are my weaknesses. According to your Word, though, I should be boasting of them so that Christ's power may rest on me. Because this is true, please teach me how to boast of my illness so that your power can be made perfect in my weakness. It is my pride that prevents me from sharing my weaknesses with my friends and fellow Christians. I pray that you will break down my pride so that I can truly have Christ's power rest in me. I pray that you will also change the attitude of my fellow Christians so that they can accept me with my mental health challenges. Help us all understand that Christ's grace truly is sufficient for all of us. I pray these things in the powerful name of Jesus, the giver of godly grace, amen.

MOVING FORWARD:

- Ask yourself if you truly believe today's Scripture—2 Corinthians 12:9—and then ask God for greater faith to believe it fully. Memorize it and meditate on it often.

- Now write down several of your weaknesses (your *weaknesses* are not your sins), including challenges that result from your mental health problems. Under your list of weaknesses, write down the words "I will boast of these. I will boast of these all the more gladly, because God's power is made perfect in my weakness." Now pray that God helps you boast of them without shame and see how Christ's power changes your life.

How often do you find yourself boasting of your strengths and your weaknesses? Who do you boast to?

FORTY-NINE
WOUNDED

"So we say with confidence, 'The Lord is my helper; I will not be afraid. What can man do to me?'"

— Hebrews 13:6

Man can actually do quite a bit of harm. Some people have such a way with words that with their bitterness and sarcasm so clearly expressed, their words can deeply pierce one's heart with great force. Others don't even need to verbalize their disapproval and disappointment; their contemptuous glances are enough to convey much anger and discontent. Although the emotions people express toward me are often less hostile than they could be, sometimes it is the subtle strikes that are most hurtful. A deep cut made quickly definitely creates great pain, but multiple cuts of smaller and shallower depths can produce pain that spreads widely to other areas. Upsetting words sprinkled here and there can multiply in toxicity over time, and their accumulated effect can sometimes cause greater harm than a one-time attack. It may very well be that people do not intend to hurt me, but nevertheless, their words and actions, when filtered through my sensitive heart, can exert significant negative effects on me. And for me, simply knowing that the scars will be healed isn't quite enough to take the actual pain away.

I can't deny the fact that pain is an unavoidable necessity of life, but I do know that there is no damage done by man that cannot be mended by the Lord, for he is my helper and defender in every attack that comes my way. The Lord has shown me that the purpose of the pain he allows isn't to hurt, destroy, or torture me, but rather, to strengthen and teach me, bringing me to greater maturity in Christ. All painful experiences are part of his marvelous plan. So really, although people are capable of causing me great grief, with God on my side, no one can take away the unquenchable joy that is found in our Lord.

PRAYER

Dear Lord,

You are my helper, and I should not be afraid. What can people do to me? It's easy to say, yet I am frequently hurt by people because of their words, attitudes, contemptuous glances, sarcasm, and disapproval of my actions. Sometimes I pretend that I am not hurt by their words and actions, but you know my pain and suffering, for nothing is hidden from you. Today I choose to accept you as my personal helper and defender in every attack that comes my way. I will not seek revenge. Instead, I choose to accept the pain as an unavoidable necessity in my life, as part of your sovereign plan. I believe and accept that all painful experiences you have allowed, and will allow, in my life have a good purpose. Their purpose is not to hurt, destroy, or torture me, but to strengthen and teach me, bringing me to greater maturity in Christ. Dear Lord, even as I struggle with my emotional pain, with you on my side, no one can take away the unquenchable joy that is found in you. I pray these things in the name of Jesus, my helper and defender, amen.

MOVING FORWARD:

- Write down three to five painful interactions

you have experienced from people in the last year, including any words said about or actions done to you.

- Next to each of these experiences, write down what emotional and physical effects they had on you. Examples could include crying, poor sleep, depressed mood, anxiety, fear, headaches, abdominal pain, social isolation, drug and alcohol abuse, and destructive behavior.
- Now open your Bible to James 1:2-4, read it, meditate on it, and ask the Lord what he is teaching you through your painful experiences. Write your reflections down next to each painful experience you listed above, and thank God for each one.

What are some ways you have been molded and matured through painful experiences you've endured? What kinds of things did you learn?

FIFTY
SCARRED

"But we have this treasure in jars of clay to show that this all-surpassing power is from God and not from us . . . We always carry around in our body the death of Jesus, so that the life of Jesus may also be revealed in our body. For we who are alive are always being given over to death for Jesus' sake, so that his life may be revealed in our mortal body."

— 2 Corinthians 4:7,10-11

Some time ago, I witnessed a beautiful sight. The sun was shining a magnificent beam of light through a small and rather unspectacular blob of cloud. Although I really couldn't find anything particularly beautiful about the little cloud itself, the glorious spectrum of colors it reflected certainly made for an exquisite and striking picture. As I marveled at how such a nondescript and plain object can be used to convey the breathtaking splendor of the sun, I thought of how astounding it is that *we*, sinful and imperfect beings, can be vessels through which *God's* unsurpassed glory is revealed. As tiny and insignificant as we may feel in this vast and enormous world, the Lord has chosen *us* to be reflectors of his beauty, carriers of his sweet aroma, and instruments to accomplish his will and his purposes.

So many times I have felt "un-usable"—weak, broken, helpless, and defeated—yet I must not forget that no matter how difficult the trials and struggles are that I'm going through or how painful and unrelenting my suffering may seem, the Lord is using me to demonstrate *his* tremendous power and ability, not mine. The transformed lives we witness, the achievements we see in ourselves and others, the countless gifts and blessings we tangibly enjoy . . . all of these are accomplished by the power of God alone. What absolute joy and privilege we have to not only be recipients of God's grace, but also to be his ambassadors to the world, telling of his glory through our words, thoughts, actions, and our most trying circumstances. We must never be discouraged by our flaws and shortcomings and thus cease to offer ourselves wholly as sacrifices to him, for God can, and does, use even the most ordinary and broken of people to make his name and glory known. How thankful and relieved I am that life is all about *God*, not me!

PRAYER

Dear God,

I often feel un-usable, weak, broken, helpless, and defeated. Thank you for showing me today that no matter how difficult my trials and struggles may be, and despite all of my suffering, you are using me to demonstrate your tremendous power and ability, not mine. Lord, it is a privilege to receive your grace and tell of your glory through my words, actions, and difficult life circumstances. I am a jar of clay with many cracks and breaks. Help me never to be discouraged by my flaws and shortcomings, though. Help me to never stop offering myself wholly as a sacrifice to you because you can, and do, use the most ordinary and broken people to make your name and glory known. I am so thankful and relieved to know that the universe is all about you, God, not me. I pray these things in the name of Jesus, the creator of the universe and my body and soul, amen.

MOVING FORWARD:

- Take a pottery class and create some pots, mugs, and other items of clay. The process of making these items will in and of itself be therapeutic. Then use some of these items or place them where you will see them often to remind yourself daily that you are a very special pot of clay, made by God himself, for a very specific purpose, for God's glory.

- Find a damaged pot, vase, mug, or any other type of container. It could be broken, cracked, not attractive, or have missing parts. Transform the damaged piece by placing something beautiful inside it, such as a flower, cactus, ribbons, fruit, jewelry, a candle, or colorful pens. As you look at it regularly, let the Holy Spirit remind you of God's beauty and glory revealed through you.

How does it feel to imagine the breathtaking splendor of God's glory being revealed through you?

FIFTY-ONE
NUMB TO SIN

"So we make it our goal to please him, whether we are at home in the body or away from it."

— 2 Corinthians 5:9

I feel like I am becoming numbed to disobeying God. Or maybe I have just forgotten what the joy that comes from living in obedience to him feels like. When trapped in a continuous pattern of sin, we try and try to somehow relieve the added tension and anxiety that accompany our behaviors. Perhaps we do this by convincing ourselves that "it's not so bad—we just need to ask for forgiveness, and all will be fine." But all *is not* fine. Disobedience to our gracious God is not something to be treated lightly. Why else would Paul exclaim "By no means!" in response to the question, "[S]hall we sin because we are not under law but under grace" (Romans 6:15)? I do not mean to heap an even greater sense of guilt on any of us, for I fully believe that the shed blood of Christ is sufficient to cover the stain of every single one of our sins. But I too need to be reminded of the blessings that are ours when we obey God, for "[b]lessed rather are those who hear the word of God and obey it" (Luke 11:28). In fact, if we are truly convinced of the love we profess for our God, we have an obligation to follow him in all we do. "If you love me, you will keep my commands" (John 14:15).

It's a fact. If we love him, we will obey him. So obey him is what we must do. Paul tells us that we are slaves to the one we obey, and we have the opportunity to choose for ourselves whom we want to obey. Do we want to be "slaves to sin, which leads to death, or to obedience, which leads to righteousness?" (Romans 6:16). This isn't too difficult a choice to make, but it *is* a bit more difficult to live out. We will fall short, no doubt about that, but let's not ever quit being slaves to our perfect and loving Master. Let's always make it our highest goal to please him wherever we are, in everything we say, think, feel, and do, for this is how we can demonstrate to him and to the world that we truly love God and treasure him above everything else.

PRAYER

Dear Heavenly Father,
Please search my heart today. Do I really love you? Do I treasure you above everything else? Do I truly obey you? Am I a slave to sin, which leads to death, or am I slave to obedience, which leads to righteousness? Am I trapped in a continuous pattern of sin? Am I treating my sin too lightly? Please forgive me and show me how to deal with my sin. I do believe that the shed blood of Jesus is sufficient to completely wash away my sins. Thank you for reminding me that the blessings you provide are mine when I obey you and not just when I believe in you. I repent of my disobedience. Please help me not to hide behind my struggles and pain, but to always express to you my weaknesses and sins. I pray this in the gracious name of Jesus, the searcher of all hearts, amen.

MOVING FORWARD:

- Kneel down and begin confessing *all* your sins. Don't hide any sin from God, regardless of how small or insignificant you may think it is. Ask the Lord to reveal how you may be hiding behind your mental illness and how it may be causing you to justify or rationalize continued sins. Confess your sins and repent before God. Repeat a prayer of repentance on a daily basis for the next two weeks, and then make it a habit for the rest of your life.

Are you trapped in a continuous pattern of sin and discouraged by your inability to be free from its hold on you? How might the practices of believing in God, repenting before God, and obeying God free you from the entanglement of sin?

FIFTY-TWO
NOT FIGHTING ALONE

"'Don't be afraid, the prophet answered. 'Those who are with us are more than those who are with them.' And Elisha prayed, 'O LORD, open his eyes so he may see.' Then the LORD opened the servant's eyes, and he looked and saw the hills full of horses and chariots of fire all around Elisha."

— 2 Kings 6:16-17

When the strength of Satan seems so powerful and overwhelming in our lives, it can be so easy for us to lose heart and waver in our faith in the *most* powerful God. When our battle with sin and weakness seems like a losing and hopeless one, the temptation to despair and give up can rob us of all joy and delight in our Lord. But let us not forget that the Lord has not left us to face our enemies alone; rather, he commands his angels to surround us, guard us, deliver us, and protect us. Although the Lord granted Elisha's servant the ability to see the massive number of heavenly hosts fighting for them, I think it is the confidence and assurance exhibited by Elisha that we need to imitate. It is very unlikely that we will physically see the invisible heavenly beings fighting alongside us in our various struggles and troubles, but let us be reminded that we have on our side the army of God conquering our enemies for us.

It isn't only sheer numbers that ensure our victory over Satan; it is the sole fact that *God is on our side*. There is no greater confidence we can gain than this truth: "If God is for us, who can be against us?" (Romans 8:31). And because of this, we must not fear. Our help comes from the Maker of heaven and earth, and *he* will make sure that we are not destroyed or defeated. All we can do is place our complete trust in his mighty, unsurpassable name—calling and crying out for his mercy and grace to fall upon us and inviting him to take his rightful place as King over every detail of our lives.

PRAYER

Dear Lord,

Because you are my God, and I am your child, my help comes from you. You are my protector and my defender, and I will not be afraid. If you are for me, who can be against me? Even though I can't see your angels fighting alongside me, help me believe that you are by my side, conquering the enemies for me. Help me to not be afraid. I pray for your mercy and grace to fall on me. I will put my complete trust in your mighty and powerful name every day, every week, and every month. You are the Lord and King over every area of my life, and my confidence is only in you. Thank you for protecting me from harm. I pray these things in the name of Jesus, my King and Protector, amen.

MOVING FORWARD:

- Every time you see any kind of fire, such as a fireplace, campfire, or a burning candle, do one of the following:
    - Remember the story of Elisha and

the chariots of fire around him protecting him from his enemies.

- Recall the unseen, but ever-present, power of God as he protects you day and night, especially during your periods of worsening mental health.
- Say the following prayer: "Lord, open my eyes to see the angels, horses and chariots of fire, that you have placed around me for my protection."

Do you believe that God protects you with one angel, several angels, or an army of angels? Why?

FIFTY-THREE
CONSTANT IN MY CHAOS

"Jesus Christ is the same yesterday and today and forever."
— Hebrews 13:8

It is so amazing to be reminded that our Lord never changes and has never changed throughout all of history. It may be easier to see him as unchanging on a day-to-day basis, for it can be difficult to notice changes even in *people* who we come in contact with every day. But sometimes I worry that the Lord may slowly change in subtle, yet significant, ways over time. Sure, he forgives, but would he still be as quick to forgive the same sins I commit and repent of over and over again after so long? Yes, he is patient, but would he not grow at least a bit tired of my incessant pleas for the same things prayer after prayer? Would he not become flustered at my inability to see past the heaviness of my own cross or my failure to raise my eyes toward the glorious prize he has waiting for me at the end of this life? No. He has not, and he will not.

The same Lord who gave his life to purchase mine has obtained for me forgiveness that covers all my sins for all time, for Christ "has appeared once for all at the culmination of the ages to do away with sin by the sacrifice of himself" (Hebrews 9:26). And are we not encouraged to "pray in the Spirit on all occasions with all kinds of prayers and requests" (Ephesians 6:18)? And don't we know that through our suffering God is developing in us perseverance that will allow us to hold fast until the end (Romans 5:3)? People may begin to withhold forgiveness from me, become weary of my continuous and tiresome complaints, or experience great frustration and disappointment with me. But the Lord will not change. His love and grace that was sufficient yesterday is still sufficient today. His forgiveness in the past still stands effective for me today, and it always will. I will change, and my understanding of him will only grow deeper, but he will always be the same perfect God I have been trusting and following since the day he first found me.

PRAYER

Thank you, Lord.
I am so glad that you have never changed throughout history. Your love, righteousness, mercy, and grace to me is the same over my entire life. You are faithful to me when I am depressed, anxious, afraid, and feel unable to cope with life. Your death on the cross has given me eternal life. Your sacrifice has obtained for me forgiveness that covers all my sins for all time. Some people withhold forgiveness from me and are weary from hearing about my struggles. But your grace and love that was sufficient for me yesterday is still sufficient for me today. Your forgiveness of my sins in the past is still complete today and always will be. I thank you for being the same perfect God I have been trusting and following since the day you first found me. I pray this in the unchanging name of Jesus, amen.

MOVING FORWARD:

- Write down a list of five to ten improved characteristics and behavioral changes you have seen over the years in your life since you became a follower of Jesus. This might include improved control over your words and language, increased patience, more unconditional love, more empathy to the sick, etc. Pray and ask God to continue to increase these.

- Write a list of five to ten characteristics in your life where you have not seen an improvement since becoming a follower of Jesus. This could include anxiety, anger control, peace in your heart, physical fitness, etc. Pray and ask God to help you change these for the better.
- Write out a list of five to ten characteristics of God that never change. This could include his love, faithfulness, protection, forgiveness, and provision for you. Thank him for them.

How much do you truly believe that Christ's forgiveness for your sins is complete, for now and forever? What can help you remember this truth?

FIFTY-FOUR
NO NEED TO QUESTION

"As for God, his way is perfect."
— 2 Samuel 22:31

Oftentimes, I am overwhelmed by my pain, hurts and sorrows, but today I am overwhelmed simply by the amazing grace of God. I am so overwhelmed by his indescribable goodness to me and for his truly perfect faithfulness to his children. His ways really are unfathomable and mysterious, aren't they?

When the darkest of storm clouds are all that fill my skies, I stand confused and perplexed at the seemingly inactive hand of God in my life. I question his goodness, I question his faithfulness, and I question the sureness of his promises. When my life seems to be made up of nothing but endless repetitions of the same mundane routine over and over again, I start to doubt the promised, abundant life that is ours in Christ. At the same time, when the joys he pours into my life continue to build and build to the point of overflowing, I am also left wondering *why* his love and grace toward me are so marvelous and incredible.

I can try, but I cannot fully understand God. All I know is that his ways are perfect, his love for me is perfect, his care for me is perfect, and *he* is altogether perfect. I do not understand why I must muddle my way through the frightening and sometimes lonely mazes of life, and I do not understand why I must traverse the dusty hills of scorching and blazing deserts. But I *do* know that he has not left me to figure my way out on my own, and I *do* know that his life-giving oasis of his water of life is always accessible to me, no matter where I may be.

PRAYER

Dear God,

When the darkest of storm clouds are all that fill my skies, and I become deeply depressed, anxious, confused, and perplexed at your seemingly inactive hand in my life, I question your goodness and faithfulness. Please forgive me for my doubts. I am imperfect in my physical, emotional, and mental health. Thank you for reminding me today that your ways are perfect, your love for me is perfect, your care for me is perfect, and you are altogether perfect. I am truly overwhelmed by your grace and love in my life. Please pour more of your grace, love, and healing onto me, in your perfect timing and in your perfect way. I ask this humbly, for your glory. I pray these things in the name of Jesus, who always answers in his perfect timing, amen.

MOVING FORWARD:

- If you can afford it, go and buy a mug with a *custom label* for your morning coffee or tea. Print the words "God's ways are perfect", and attach these words somewhere on the cup. Drink from that cup whenever you question

God's ways in your life and his goodness toward you. Every time you read the phrase, "God's ways are perfect," thank God for his perfect love, grace, mercy, care, and healing in your life, especially regarding your physical and mental health.

If God's ways are perfect, and our ways are not, how should we respond to the storm clouds that come our way?

FIFTY-FIVE
VIEW FROM ABOVE

"It is God who arms me with strength
and makes my way secure.
He makes my feet like the feet of a deer;
he causes me to stand on the heights."
— 2 Samuel 22:33-34

I have never been one to be afraid of heights, but I do wonder why being high above the ground can be frightening for so many people. Perhaps it is the lack of confidence people have in the structure or place they are standing on, fearing it may somehow collapse and fail to support them. Still others may be afraid of the possibility of falling. Someone once told me that he becomes extremely queasy when looking down from any considerable height because he fears he might lose control, topple over a fence or barrier, and ultimately fall.

The heights upon which *God* enables us to stand are not ones we should fear. They are heights to which we are lifted so high that God protects us from drowning in rising waves of distress, sorrow, and confusion. These heights allow us to view our circumstances with wider and broader perspectives, and they prevent us from being dragged into the worries and cares of this world. God provides us with the sure ability to stand firm in the freedom he has given us and allows us to see his unfailing love and care for us through vigilant eyes of faith. Just like the deer that gracefully leaps and springs across the plains, we too can be confident God will give us the strength and wisdom to stand and run courageously, without wobbling or stumbling, on his safe and beautiful heights.

PRAYER

Dear God,
I am often afraid of what you are doing with me and where you are taking me. The heights you take me to should not be ones that cause me fear. You lift me up to protect me from drowning in rising waves of distress, sorrow, and confusion. Thank you. When I am with you and lifted up, I see my circumstances from your wider and broader perspective. Thank you. Please help me see my life from the right perspective (i.e. your perspective). You are my God who arms me with strength and makes my way perfect. You are my God who makes my feet like the feet of a deer, who enables me to stand on safe and beautiful heights. Please help me and protect me. I pray all this in the name of Jesus, my protector, amen.

MOVING FORWARD:

- Take a drive to a lookout point in your city such as a mountain or one of the tall buildings. As you look at your city, notice that you now have a different perspective of the city and life itself. Allow that view to help you understand that God has a bigger perspective of your life than you do. Ask God to help you always see your life, including your mental health problems, from his point of view.

- During times of discouragement, go back to the lookout point to remind yourself of God's perspective.

When have your thanked God for arming you with strength, making your way perfect, making your feet like the feet of a deer, and enabling you to stand on the heights?

FIFTY-SIX
UNDESERVING

"Who am I, O Sovereign LORD . . . that you have brought me this far?"

— 2 Samuel 7:18

Honestly, who am I to complain to the Lord about how frustrated I am of my seemingly endless struggles and suffering? Of course, it is out of immense pain that I demand an explanation from him, but what if I turn my questions around? Instead of asking why this pain remains, what if I ask him why so much grace has been poured onto me and why I have been protected and kept safe all this time? If I asked him this, I think the simple answer would be that it is because he loves me. We must remember that our God is gracious and merciful to his children, compassionate to the hurting, just and righteous in all his ways, and always faithful to his promises to us. He is all-powerful, all-knowing, his truths all-encompassing, and always present in every situation, everywhere. Out of his sovereignty he has chosen me, created me, and saved me, and he desires to refine me according to his good purposes. God has brought me safely thus far because he has promised to carry to completion his work of sanctification in me. He is a God who is able to and *will* keep me from falling. He will present me before his glorious throne without fault and with great joy (Jude 24).

These truths are sufficient to fully answer all the questions I can ever come up with, be they questions about my joys or sorrows, my easy or hard times. They leave me completely humbled and feeling tiny and small, but this is precisely the place where I should be. Realizing my deep need for and utter dependence on God is where I can begin to come to terms with my circumstances. I may not fully understand all the intricate details of his plans for me, but I do know this: every breath I take and every pleasant and unpleasant moment I experience is a gift given by this indescribable Lord whom I have described. Because he desires to work nothing but *good* for my life, I know that it is his grace and strength alone that has sustained and will continue to sustain me, no matter what comes my way.

PRAYER

Dear Lord,

Sometimes I feel like a big complainer; I often complain about my seemingly endless struggles and suffering. Please forgive me. Why do you love me so much? Why do you protect me and keep me safe? Who am I that you have chosen me, created me, saved me from hell, and given me the gifts of your Holy Spirit and eternal life? Thank you for promising to complete the work of sanctification in me. I believe your promise that you will present me before your glorious throne without fault and with great joy. My mental health problems leave me completely humbled and feeling tiny and small, allowing me to realize my deep need for and utter dependence on you. Your desire is to work nothing but good in my life. Your grace and strength alone have sustained me and will continue to sustain me, no matter what trials will come my way. Thank you. I pray these things in the loving and sovereign name of Jesus my Lord, amen.

MOVING FORWARD:

- Write down this verse twenty times: "Who am I, O sovereign Lord, that you have brought me this far?"

- After writing *each* sentence, thank God for his goodness and faithfulness to you. Remind yourself each time that his love for you is perfect, eternal, and not something you can, or have to, earn.

Have you ever counted how many times you complain to God and people in an average day? How might you acknowledge and express your frustrations about your suffering in a healthy way, while still focusing on the goodness and faithfulness of God to you?

FIFTY-SEVEN
SLIPPED FROM YOUR TRUTHS

"Stand firm then, with the belt of truth buckled around your waist."

— Ephesians 6:14

My heart and mind rarely demand evidence to ascertain whether my feelings and thoughts are helpful or harmful given a situation. Even though some may view my emotions to be inappropriate or irrational, these feelings nevertheless impact me deeply and sometimes in quite intense ways. But God graciously allows me to know that how I feel often contradicts with what I know to be true in my mind. I know that I'm loved by him even when I feel unloved. I know that he sees me as a child of worth even when I feel worthless. I know he has forgiven all of my sins even though I feel guilty of my various behaviors time after time. I know he wants to protect me from all harm even as I feel like I want to harm myself.

I need to remember that it is his truth, not my

feelings, that will ultimately reign. I am very often far too easily swayed by my emotions that reflect lies and twisted truths. I then conclude that if how I feel doesn't correspond with what I know, my knowledge must be flawed in some way. But while God has given us emotions to experience and use, I don't think he intends for us to rely on emotions to be the sole determinant of truth. "Jesus answered, 'I am the way and the truth and the life'" (John 14:6). It can be a frightening thing, but I must learn to develop a critical eye for my feelings and start to truly believe and trust the truths that God has revealed and made known to me. "The LORD is near to all who call on him, to all who call on him in truth" (Psalm 145:18). He himself is the truth, and it is that truth I need near me at all times. Without him, how else can I possibly fight against the destructive lies that threaten to break and defeat me?

PRAYER

Dear Lord God,

Thank you for creating me in your image, able to experience powerful emotions. Thank you for being the truth and helping me understand the truth. Please forgive me for often allowing my emotions to lead me astray from the truth. Please help me to integrate your truths with my emotions, bringing you glory and honor. May your Holy Spirit guide me to develop a critical eye for my feelings and help me fully believe the truths you have revealed to me through your Word. I often experience strong emotions that lead me to make choices that are destructive. Today I pray that you change my feelings of depression and anxiety to joy and peace as I call on you in truth. I pray these things in the name of the God of truth, Jesus, amen.

MOVING FORWARD:

- Write down three emotions that usually produce positive and helpful behaviors in you. Examples may include joy, love, kindness, and contentment.
- Write down three emotions that usually lead

to harmful and destructive behaviors. Examples may include fear, anxiety, depression, greed, and anger.

- Now remind yourself that you have a *choice* as to how you will respond and act when you experience different emotions every day and that your choices should be based on truth from God's Word, not lies and half-truths from the world.

Are you truly aware that even as you struggle through mental health problems, the choice of which truths you believe and how you manage your emotions can be in your control? How might this truth help you cope with harmful thoughts and painful emotions?

FIFTY-EIGHT
WILL I EVER BE OKAY?

"Surely it was for my benefit
that I suffered such anguish.
In your love you kept me
from the pit of destruction;
you have put all my sins
behind your back."

— Isaiah 38:17

I am deeply thankful for the times when God lets me know for certain that he has everything under control, and things will be okay. One day. There are moments when he allows me to catch a small glimpse of the glorious future he has in store for us. He fills me with an indescribable hope for the day when he will finally restore all things to the way they should be. It is true that I read about his promises for an eternity that is free of all pain and suffering, but still he graciously covers me with a deep reassurance that there indeed *will* be an end to all the hurt that I am experiencing.

I may not know the reasons God has in bringing

me through this dark valley of grief, but whatever they may be, I truly do believe that this pain can be for my benefit. If I have doubts about this, then I need to consider how faithful God has been in every single step I have taken along this road. If he ordained for me to suffer so that I would fall into complete ruin, I doubt I would still be here right now declaring the greatness of his grace and mercy. The reason why he has brought me to this time of anguish is the same reason why he will surely keep me from the pit of despair—it is because *he loves me*. "But God disciplines us for our good, that we may share in his holiness. No discipline seems pleasant at the time, but painful. Later on, however, it produces a harvest of righteousness and peace for those who have been trained by it" (Hebrews 12:10-11). No matter how much we have suffered and how much more we will have to suffer, we have to remember this: *The Lord disciplines those he loves* (Hebrews 12:6), and we must "[e]ndure hardship as discipline" (Hebrews 12:7). We may feel as if we are nearing the pit of destruction, but know this: because we are safe and secure in his love, he will *never* let us fall too far.

PRAYER

Dear Heavenly Father,

Thank you for the reminder that you have everything under control and that things will be okay, especially regarding my mental health. You have forgiven me of my sins because I have repented of them. In your love, you have kept me from the pit of destruction, yet have allowed me to suffer anguish for my own benefit. Please graciously cover me with a deep reassurance that there indeed will be an end to all the hurt that I am experiencing. I am convinced that you love me dearly and that your discipline is for my good, allowing me to share in your holiness. Help me never to forget that you discipline those whom you love. As I walk through these trials, I will endure hardship as discipline, knowing that it will produce a harvest of righteousness and peace. I pray these things in the loving name of Jesus, amen.

MOVING FORWARD:

- Write down the following phrases and say them out aloud several times until you truly believe them:

- I will endure hardship as discipline from the Lord.
- The Lord disciplines those whom he loves.
- The Lord loves me.

What reasons has your Heavenly Father shown you as to why he is allowing you to go through this present dark valley of grief?

FIFTY-NINE
WORN

"Do you not know?
Have you not heard?
The LORD is the everlasting God,
the Creator of the ends of the earth.
He will not grow tired or weary,
and his understanding no one can fathom.
He gives strength to the weary
and increases the power of the weak.
Even youths grow tired and weary,
and young men stumble and fall;
but those who hope in the LORD
will renew their strength.
They will soar on wings like eagles;
they will run and not grow weary,
they will walk and not be faint."

— Isaiah 40:28-31

Sometimes I grow so tired and weary. Actually, I feel tired and weary the majority of the time. I continually ask the Lord, whatever happened to the promise of running and not growing weary, of walking and not being faint? But why do I ask? Nothing has changed. The promise is still the same; God is still the same. My God never becomes fatigued; he exists and endures from everlasting to everlasting. These words remind us that although we will become worn, we will become exhausted, and we will become drained, the Lord always refreshes and restores, providing us with strength and power to continue running this race of life for him.

In order to *restore* or *renew* anything, something has to have become "old" or broken in some way, doesn't it? There may be many answers for why I am not yet flying like eagles without the burdens and weights I presently carry, but perhaps I simply need to let my stumbling and falling run their course, all the while holding firmly onto the promise that God will make me new in his time. And truly, the further I fall, the more glorious it will be when my loving Savior finally draws me up from the depths of sorrow and into his unending, eternal joy. The Lord understands me in ways far greater than I can know, so let me not lose hope, for one day he will mend my every bruise, chip, and wound, restoring me to wholeness once again.

PRAYER

Dear Lord,

I am feeling tired and weary most of the time. Your Word speaks to me today and reminds me that "Even youths grow tired and weary." Only you do not grow tired and weary, and only you can increase the power of the weak. I confess that I am tired and weak because I struggle with overwhelming stress, depression, anxiety, insomnia, and feelings of hopelessness. Teach me how to hope in you Lord so that you can renew my strength. I want to soar on wings like eagles; I want to run and not grow weary; I want to walk and not be faint. As you restore and renew me, take away what is old and broken. Remove the burdens and weights I presently carry and help me trust in you and your promises. Jesus, you are my strength and my hope. I commit myself to continue running the race set before me as long as you continue to give me your strength and your power. I pray this in the everlasting name of Jesus, amen.

MOVING FORWARD:

- List three behaviors and habits that are "broken," "old," and need renewing. Examples might include anger, a thankless attitude, grumbling, poor eating habits, lack of exercise, irregular church attendance, infrequent prayer, and others.

- Give up these broken and old habits and lay them at the feet of Jesus, asking him to replace them with new and healthy habits such as a grateful attitude, thankfulness, regular church attendance, prayer and Bible reading, healthy eating habits, adequate sleep, and proper exercise.
- Work together with someone such as your doctor, counselor, or pastor in order to make these changes.
- Combine spiritual and physical disciplines as you seek healing and restoration from the Lord.

What helps you hold firmly onto the promise of God that he is able to make you new in his time?

SIXTY
HOW MUCH LONGER?

"He said to them: 'It is not for you to know the times or dates the Father has set by his own authority.'"

— Acts 1:7

Now why not? I can't help but think that if only I knew when Christ is returning, then the rest of this life would be so much easier to get through. If I only had a specific goal to "work toward," then my days might be a bit easier to endure. So why can't he just tell us? Why does he have to leave us in suspense?

Rather than merely looking forward to the *day* itself, perhaps he desires for us to burn with a deep passion and longing for *him*. Perhaps God conceals from us the details of his return so that we would always be vigilant and watchful, waiting in eager anticipation for that glorious day of the Lord. It can be hard for someone like myself, who *just wants to know*, to accept the fact that sometimes, some details are not the most important thing. We see in part, but we *will* see in full.

We know in part, but we *will* know in full. For now, he has told us all we need to faithfully carry out the work he has ordained for us. He is coming soon enough, and he is coming for sure.

Even though we may not know exactly when we will finally see our Lord, we must never forget that he *is* returning and hence we *must* live in light of this truth. "But you, brothers, are not in darkness so that this day should surprise you like a thief. You are all sons of the light and sons of the day. We do not belong to the night or to the darkness. So then, let us not be like others, who are asleep, but let us be alert and self-controlled. For those who sleep, sleep at night, and those who get drunk, get drunk at night. But since we belong to the day, let us be self-controlled, putting on faith and love as a breastplate, and the hope of salvation as a helmet" (1 Thessalonians 5:4-8).

PRAYER

Dear Heavenly Father,
I have not thought about your second coming for a long time. Please help me remember regularly that you are coming back to earth soon. You are going to take me home to heaven to be with you. In my depression, anxiety, stress, and addictions, I often can't look ahead toward the future. I frequently concentrate on my own immediate problems rather than on the treasure that is ahead, prepared by you, as my free gift. Help me to be vigilant and watchful, waiting in eager anticipation for that glorious day of your return. I am not living in darkness, and your return will not surprise me like a thief. I am a child of the light and a child of the day. Help me to be self-controlled, putting on faith and love as a breastplate and the hope of salvation as a helmet. I pray this in the name of my King, Jesus, who is coming back to earth soon, amen.

MOVING FORWARD:

- Write out the following two commandments given to us in Scripture by apostle Paul in Colossians 3:1-4. Place it where you can read it every day for the next week.

- *Commandment 1*: "Since then, you have been raised with Christ, sets your heart on things above, where Christ is, seated at the right hand of God." (Colossians 3:1)
- *Commandment 2*: "Set your minds on things that are above, not on earthly things. For you died, and your life is hidden with Christ in God. When Christ, who is your life, appears, then you also will appear with him in glory." (Colossians 3:2-4)

How can you turn your mind to think more about the things of heaven than the things of earth?

SIXTY-ONE
EVEN ME

"When they saw the courage of Peter and John and realized that they were unschooled, ordinary men, they were astonished and they took note that these men had been with Jesus."

— Acts 4:13

You know, we really do not need to be the smartest, most special, nor most popular people in order to deeply impact and influence the world with the message of God. On the contrary, what we need is a servant's heart and an appropriately humble attitude to loudly declare the goodness of God to a watching and skeptical world. People don't need to see how intelligent we are or how righteous we try to make ourselves out to be; what they must see is the power of God at work in our lives.

I believe this can take place only when we seek to draw, and remain, close to our Lord. Although the crowd was taken aback by the courage Peter and John displayed, it is very likely that by putting two and two together, the people were able to conclude that the disciples were empowered by none other than the one with whom they had spent much time with—Jesus Christ.

Do people look at our actions and conclude that we are only able to accomplish what we accomplish because of the grace that the Lord so abundantly bestows upon us? Do we give all honor and glory to him, or do we save a bit of the glory for ourselves? Our lives must not be lived to achieve the selfish end of exalting ourselves; we are on a mission to spread the love of God to a dying, perishing world. Let this always be our prayer: "Not to us, O LORD, not to us but to your name be the glory" (Psalm 115:1).

PRAYER

Dear Lord,

I suffer from a mental illness and can't imagine how I can impact and influence my family, friends, and neighborhood, let alone the world, with the message of God. Please teach me that I am a child of God, and the Holy Spirit is in me, so that I am able to declare the goodness of God in a very powerful way. Please help me to have a servant's heart and a humble attitude as I reflect the love and grace of Jesus. As people thank me, teach me to give the thanks to you; as people praise me, teach me to give all the praise to you; as people honor me, teach me to give the honor to you. Not to us, O LORD, not to us, but to your name be the glory. I pray these things in the name of Jesus, my Lord, who deserves all glory and honor and praise forever, amen.

MOVING FORWARD:

- Read the two books by Dr. John MacArthur called *Twelve Ordinary Men* and *Twelve Extraordinary Women.* You will see how God can use ordinary people with character flaws, illnesses, poor education, and in poverty to change the world. You will read how God turned their weakness into strength, producing greatness out of that which seems lowly and unworthy.

How has God changed you day by day and used you to influence part of the world for his glory?

SIXTY-TWO
GOING MY OWN WAY

"Leave these men alone! Let them go! For if their purpose or activity is of human origin, it will fail. But if it is from God, you will not be able to stop these men; you will only find yourselves fighting against God."

— Acts 5:38-39

Fighting against God. No doubt this is a losing battle for us. Yet how often do we fight against the will of God without actually realizing it? I know for myself, I can become so caught up and tightly wrapped up in my own desires and plans that I neglect to step back and seek *first* the counsel of the Lord. After all, I've already put much deliberation and thought into my plans, and they already seem so perfect and flawless, how could God *possibly* have anything different to say?

I find it such a tragedy the amount of time I have wasted venturing away from the Lord, going my own way, and failing to depend on his guidance in my decisions and choices. Rather than asking him to conform my will to his and align my desires with his, all I can sometimes do is half-heartedly pray that he would approve of mine. But God isn't merely a higher order official signing permission slips for his children; he longs to enlighten our hearts and minds with the things of God, teaching us to desire the things he desires, value the things he values, and love the things he loves. I must remember that the ultimate reason for every decision I make and every action I take is to fulfill the purposes of God. In my confusion and uncertainty, who can provide advice and instruction more sound than God himself? Time after time and circumstance after circumstance, he continues to reveal to me just how much higher his ways are than mine.

There truly is no wiser choice for us than to fully surrender and submit to the will of God. Unlike ours, *his* plans cannot be frustrated, *his* ways cannot be thwarted, *his* battles will never be lost, and most importantly, *his* decisions are always the very, very best. Let's not clutter our minds with self-centered thoughts and ideas. Let us make room for nothing else but the beautiful and glorious truths and wisdom of God.

PRAYER

Dear God,

I am often wrapped up in my own desires and plans. I usually make my plans without first seeking you. Please forgive me. As I become depressed, I fail to seek your guidance, and I often ask you to simply approve my selfish desires. Teach me how to seek your will, and show me how to align my desires with yours. Teach me to value the things you value, desire the things you desire, and love the things you love. Remind me daily, as I struggle with my anxiety, addictions, eating disorder, and fears that the ultimate reason for every decision I make and every action I take is to fulfill your purpose, not mine. Your plans cannot be frustrated, your ways cannot be thwarted, and your battles will never be lost. Today I repent of my pride and selfishness and fully surrender to your will. I pray these things in the name of Jesus, my sovereign and wise God, amen.

MOVING FORWARD:

- Write down the things that the Bible teaches are things God loves. Now ask God to help you love the same things. Here are some suggestions: humility, obedience, repentance, grace, mercy, giving to the poor, sharing the gospel with the unsaved, forgiving others, worshiping God in music, song, and prayer, visiting the sick, helping widows, and loving your enemies.

- If you are faced with a decision you need to make, consider the things on this list and ask the Lord to guide you to make your decision in accordance with his will.

When was the last time you asked God what he wanted from you, rather than what you wanted from him?

SIXTY-THREE
CAN'T WALK THIS ROAD ALONE

"When he [Barnabas] arrived and saw what the grace of God had done, he was glad and encouraged them all to remain true to the Lord with all their hearts. He was a good man, full of the Holy Spirit and faith, and a great number of people were brought to the Lord."

— Acts 11:23-24

It is truly a wonderful blessing to have spiritually mature, Christian mentors in our lives—people to direct us to the Lord when we feel directionless, encourage us when we become discouraged, warn us when our feet wander from the path of truth, and serve as godly models exemplifying the love of Christ for us. As I read about the fruitful work of Barnabas and the many who were brought to the Lord through his faithfulness and Spirit-filled living, I cannot help but think how many of us miss out on the blessings that can be ours when we seek accountability and guidance from the mature believers God has placed in our lives.

No matter how diligent we may feel we are in striving to obey and please the Lord with our decisions and actions, on our own we can too easily misunderstand or misinterpret the will of God. The rebuking and correcting we may cringe to receive are sometimes the very things we cannot go without, Imperfect as they may be, when we are surrounded by individuals who are faithful and unafraid to boldly teach the Word of God, I suspect that we will get our fair share of the "loving admonishing" we undoubtedly need.

Notice also that Barnabas himself was encouraged when he witnessed the grace of God that was evident in the people's lives. Not only can *we* be encouraged by the faith of our spiritual mentors, but the continual work of God in our lives may also, in fact, be a source of joy for *all* of us. I have so often found the passion and fire of newly born-again believers to be a tremendously powerful testimony to the goodness of God, and I frequently see my own faith being strengthened when witnessing the sure hand of the Lord working amazing things in their lives.

Whatever form it may take, mentorship seems to be a beautiful way of experiencing the grace of God in our lives. We were not meant to walk our spiritual journeys on our own, so may we truly grow to become "full of goodness, filled with knowledge and competent to instruct one another" (Romans 15:14). Perhaps one day, we can then use our experiences to nurture and encourage our brothers and sisters in their lives of faith with our Lord.

PRAYER

Dear Heavenly Father,

Thank you for the people you have placed in my life as mentors to discipline, rebuke, and encourage me. Thank you for my parents, teachers, coaches, pastors, counselors, doctors, relatives, and friends. Some of them have been kind, gentle, and full of grace and love, and some may not have always acted in these ways. Your Holy Spirit brought people into my life who have shared the gospel of Jesus with me and led me to a saving relationship with Christ. I thank you for them. There may be those who have hurt me and caused me much pain and suffering. You used them for good in my life anyway. I forgive them, and I thank you for them. Now, please send me more mentors who can help me through my current stage of life as I suffer with my mental health issues. I need godly people to help me grow to become full of goodness and complete in knowledge so that I can encourage others to grow in their faith in Christ. In the name of my heavenly shepherd and mentor, Jesus, amen.

MOVING FORWARD:

- Write down three people who have had an important positive influence in your life.
- If possible, thank them by phone, email, or regular mail.
- Pray and ask God to send you a God-fearing mentor for the next year.
- Ask your pastor to set up a mentorship program in your church.

What steps can you take to develop a relationship with a positive, Christian mentor in your life?

SIXTY-FOUR
BE NEAR ME, OH GOD

"He marked out their appointed times in history and the boundaries of their lands. God did this so that men would seek him and perhaps reach out for him and find him, though he is not far from each one of us. For in him we live and move and have our being."

— Acts 17:26-28

Even though I'm not a child anymore, I am still afraid of being separated from people and getting lost in crowded places. Many times, I have held conversations with friends while trying to navigate my way through busy crowds, soon realizing that they have disappeared and been carried away by swarms of people. To speak not of the embarrassment I feel when I am found carrying on a conversation with myself, I automatically become greatly anxious and worried. I have the full capability and means of finding my way home, and I do know these friends are not far, but nevertheless, there is still that sudden moment of insecurity upon discovering that I am now left to walk all alone.

Often I feel the same about God. I know he is never far from me—I *live*, *move*, and *am* in him. But sometimes I feel quite the opposite. Sometimes I too have to plead, "Do not be far from me, my God; come quickly, God, to help me" (Psalm 71:12). I must remember that the Lord is omnipresent and has promised that he will never leave me. There is absolutely no sound basis for my feelings of estrangement from God. He *isn't* far from me, and he *is* coming to help me.

You know, my disappearing friends can be quickly found if I would only lay aside my panic, turn to my other side, and find that they are still there fighting through the crowd alongside me. In a far greater way, not only is my God *right there* with me as I struggle through this life, but his steadfast love also *always* surrounds me on every side. "Seek the LORD while he may be found; call on him while he is near" (Isaiah 55:6). Even though I may not always feel it, I must trust that he *is* there. I just need to reach out for him, for I will certainly find him.

PRAYER

Dear Lord,

I often feel alone and separated from people and you. In the midst of my mental illness, I feel very lonely and often afraid. Thank you for reminding me today that you promise never to leave me nor forsake me; you are always with me and in me; you are the vine, and I am a branch attached to you; in you, I live and move and have my being. As soon as I say "Lord" or "Heavenly Father," you are listening and caring for my needs. Today I need you as a friend by my side so that I can feel your love, compassion, and peace. As I struggle through this life, may your steadfast love surround me on every side. Even though I will not always feel it, I will trust that you are there. I will seek you while you can be found and call on you while you are near. I pray this in the steadfast name of Jesus, amen.

MOVING FORWARD:

- Write out a list of times and places when you feel the Lord is near. Seek God especially during those times and in those places. Consider the following list:

    - In church, walking alone on the beach or in a forest, early in the morning at sunrise, sitting quietly in a doctor's waiting room, when reading your Bible, when you are doing devotions.
    - During special times of celebration such as Easter, Christmas, baptisms, communion services, prayer meetings, and times of worship.
- Think of tokens from or reminders of these places and situations that you can carry with you daily to help you remember that the Lord is always near and your present help at all times. For example: a leaf from a forest, a photo of your favorite sunrise, a communion cup, etc.

When and where do you feel that the Lord is closest to you and able to be found?

SIXTY-FIVE
FINDING HOPE

"Hope deferred makes the heart sick,
but a longing fulfilled is a tree of life."
— Proverbs 13:12

There are so many days when I can't help but lose sight of my hope. I see myself going through endless cycles of distress and pain, feeling completely helpless and consumed. I see myself making the same mistakes again and again, lost as to how I can possibly break free from all this. I have the great hope of an eternity spent with my Savior, and this should surely be enough encouragement for me to persevere through all circumstances. But somehow, I still *feel* hopeless. I have hope, but the fulfillment of that hope seems so far away—hope deferred really does make me feel sick.

"Yet this I call to mind and therefore I have hope: Because of the LORD's great love we are not consumed, for his compassions never fail. They are new every morning" (Lamentations 3:21-23). Knowing that I need to witness more present displays of fulfilled promises, God sprinkles my life with little instances of longings satisfied, assuring me that he truly is faithful and never fails. Bit by bit, with each demonstration of his love, he plants in my spirit of desolation a tree of reassurance, a tree of renewed trust, a tree of rekindled joy . . .

Although the fulfillment of my ultimate hope has yet to take place, the Lord really does sustain me according to his promise. He graciously allows me to catch glimpses of his works in progress and proves himself absolutely trustworthy and faithful. I remember the story of Hansel and Gretel and the breadcrumbs they used to mark their travelled path. In a similar way, to direct me, remind me, and prevent me from turning away, the Lord sets in my path little reminders of his faithfulness and goodness.

My hope in the Lord is not simply an attempt to "think positive"; it is founded on the sure promises of my unchanging God. No matter how far off my hope seems to be, I must not lose heart, for I know that "hope does not disappoint us, because God has poured out his love into our hearts by the Holy Spirit, whom he has given us" (Romans 5:5, BSB). I will one day see the fulfillment of this hope—guaranteed.

PRAYER

Dear Lord,

I keep experiencing endless cycles of distress and pain. I make the same mistakes again and again, not knowing how I can break free. Somehow I feel hopeless even though I claim to have hope in my Savior. I have hope, but the fulfillment of that hope seems so far away, and that makes my heart sick. Lord, plant in my spirit of desolation a tree of reassurance, a tree of renewed trust, a tree of rekindled joy, a tree of life. Remind me daily of the work you are doing in me so that I will never forget how trustworthy and faithful you are to me. Teach me how to not just "think positive," but to ground my hope on the pure promises of my unchanging God. Your compassions for me never fail, and they are new every morning. Forgive me for losing hope regarding the relief of my emotional pain, and give me the grace I need to trust you for the ultimate fulfillment that will soon take place in heaven with you. Guaranteed. My hope is only in you, Lord. I pray these things in the faithful name of Jesus, amen.

MOVING FORWARD:

- Write down one or two areas of your life

where you keep falling into an endless cycle of repeated struggles. For example, recurrent anxiety over various life situations, addictions such as to alcohol and pornography, explosions of anger, repeated actions of self-harm, and recurrent use of harmful language.

- Ask yourself if you have lost hope in overcoming these difficulties.
- If your answer is "yes, I have lost hope," then:
    - Read today's devotional again.
    - Pray today's prayer again.
    - Call a close friend who would be willing to spend part of a day praying and fasting with you regarding your needs.
    - Remind yourself daily that even when you fail, God's promises are still sure.

When you find yourself losing hope due to overwhelming pain and struggles, how can you remember to call to mind the eternal, unfailing hope you have in the Lord?

SIXTY-SIX
SORROWS CONCEALED

"Even in laughter the heart may ache."

— Proverbs 14:13

Doesn't this sound rather pessimistic and bleak? That although we may appear joyful in our outward expressions, our hearts may in fact be weeping with sorrow? Sometimes as I walk through the hallways of our workplace and our church, I wonder about the actual emotions felt by all the laughing people I see. Does their laughter sincerely reflect genuine joy, or is it used as a mask to conceal hidden shame and pain? I admit that I very well may be over-scrutinizing people's displays of gladness, but I do so because I too play this game of masquerade. Of course, I can produce genuine laughter at good jokes or absurd situations, but I think I am beginning to become rather skilled at "faking it." Apparently, people are able to distinguish "real" smiles from "fake" ones, with "real" ones being unique in that they involve the contraction of an additional set of muscles. There is the secret: squint your eyes a bit while pulling up the corners of your mouth. I am sure many people would be convinced.

Clearly, my purpose is not to describe strategies to fool people or cover up pain. I guess I simply want to say that although there shouldn't be a need for us to mask our hurts with imitated laughter, efforts towards real joy can, in fact, be met with success. There have been times when my pretended delight has transformed into true joy, and fake smiles have somehow turned into genuine ones. This is what the Lord declares: "I will turn their mourning into gladness; I will give them comfort and joy instead of sorrow" (Jeremiah 31:13).

God's will isn't for us to become stuck in sadness and depression; rather, he wants us to find and dwell in the full, complete joy that is found only in him. No matter how real or fake or joyful or sorrowful we may feel at any given moment, we cannot give up seeking this pure joy that our Lord offers us. And let's be greatly encouraged that one day, the Lord will take away all pain, and bestow upon us true joy and gladness that will last forever and that cannot be taken away.

PRAYER

Dear Lord,
Please search my heart. Am I truly honest about the outward expression of my emotions, or am I masquerading? Is my laughter genuine, and are my tears real? I want to be true and honest before you and people. Forgive me where I have not been genuine and honest. You know me and fully understand me, and there is nothing I can hide from you. You are able to turn my mourning into gladness and my sorrow into comfort and joy. Give me true genuine laughter, and let me live and experience complete joy that is found in you, even through these dark and deep valleys. Help me seek the pure joy that only you can provide. Your Word promises me that in heaven, there will be no more sorrow and no more emotional pain. But you also promise that tremendous joy can be found here on earth in Christ. Help me now to find that joy and express it for your glory. I pray this in the name of Jesus, the One in whom joy is found, amen.

MOVING FORWARD:

- List three to five areas of your life where you

seek joy. Examples may be friends, marriage, grandchildren, vacations, sports, cars, fashion, entertainment, or your work.

- Ask yourself if Christ is on that list.
- Be honest and ask yourself if you have truly found long-lasting, deep joy.
- Talk to the spiritual leaders at your church and ask them to help you set up a plan to obtain biblical joy through a deeper relationship with Christ.

Have you ever done an in-depth study of the words "happiness" and "joy" from a biblical perspective? What differences between the two words have you discovered?

SIXTY-SEVEN
SAFELY HIDDEN

"For you died, and your life is now hidden with Christ in God."
— Colossians 3:3

Someone once gave me an analogy of what a life hidden in Christ can look like. If our lives are imagined to be like a piece of walnut nestled snugly within the sturdy shell of God, anything that attempts to strike us must first pass through our protective shield. There is no fear of a "surprise attack" on our lives because every single part of us is well-covered and securely sheltered. Furthermore, this shield doesn't only enclose us when trouble comes; we are always hidden inside, protected and sealed by the saving blood of Christ. Wherever we may walk each day, we can constantly remain at rest within God's love and protection. There is absolutely no need to fear because he always goes before us, paving a path we are only capable of treading with him as our guide.

I am so thankful that the Lord has hidden my life in him. All my darkness and sin has been covered and washed away by his shed blood, and I have been granted the privilege of being clothed by the Lord Jesus Christ himself. "You were taught, with regard to your former way of life, to put off your old self, which is being corrupted by its deceitful desires; to be made new in the attitude of your minds; and to put on the new self, created to be like God in true righteousness and holiness" (Ephesians 4:22-24). Without his cloak of righteousness, mercy, and grace wrapped around my sinful self, there is no part of me that is not deserving of condemnation, mocking, and scorn. But now, having been redeemed by the Lord himself, there is no part of me that does not rejoice with thanksgiving and praise to my merciful and gracious Savior.

The very first thing that meets one's eyes in a walnut is the shell. In a similar way, if I have put off my old self and put on the righteous "shell" of God, then what others see should not be my failures and shortcomings; rather, they should see the wonderful fruit of the Lord's miraculous work in me. No longer do I need to walk under the heaviness of my shame; I must now devote my every step to glorifying the God who has granted me access into this amazing grace in which I now stand (Romans 5:2), letting his beauty shine forth in every place I go and through everything I do.

PRAYER

Dear God,

Thank you for dying on the cross for me, in my place, to save me from the consequences of my sins. My life is now hidden with Christ in you, dear God. All of my darkness and sin has been washed away by your shed blood, and I have been granted the privilege of being clothed by the Lord Jesus Christ himself. Because of my mental health struggles, I often walk and live in fear and shame. Thank you for reminding me today that my anxiety and depression are wrapped in your cloak of righteousness, and my addictions and other difficulties are hidden with Christ in you, Father. No longer will I walk under the heaviness of my shame; I will devote my every step to glorifying you because you have granted me your amazing grace in which I now stand. In the freeing name of Jesus, I pray, amen.

MOVING FORWARD:

- Buy a whole walnut, chestnut, or any other nut with its full shell. Place it on your desk, kitchen table, or nightstand where you can see it regularly. Every time you see it, remind yourself that you have died, and your life (including your mental health problems) is now hidden with Christ in God. Thank God every time you are reminded of this truth.

Describe the joy and comfort you feel knowing the biblical truth that you have not only died with Christ but have also been raised with him.

SIXTY-EIGHT
WEIGHT OF THIS WAIT

"When Christ, who is your life, appears, then you also will appear with him in glory."

— Colossians 3:4

I often say that I long for Christ to return really, really soon so that he can make all things right again. But I sometimes forget that when he appears, I too will appear with him *in glory*. What would it be like to be fully immersed in and wrapped by the glory of God? I imagine I would perhaps be overwhelmed, speechless, stunned, and awestruck. The astonishing truth that I will be with Christ in glory is difficult enough to comprehend in and of itself. How can I possibly grasp the full measure of the glory in which we will dwell?

If I have trouble trying to picture just how awe-inspiring that future glory will be, maybe this will help: "For our light and momentary troubles are achieving for us an eternal glory that far outweighs them all" (2

Corinthians 4:17). My troubles right now *hardly* seem "light and momentary"—in fact, they seem to be so incredibly *heavy* and never-ending. But that is precisely the point, isn't it? The eternal glory that we will live in *far* outweighs the troubles I'm facing right now. I may think that my temporary struggles are immense and great, but that eternal glory will be even more vast and immeasurable than they are. And it is these very troubles that are preparing me for that which is now unimaginable, unfathomable, and indescribable. So let me look forward in eager anticipation for the glory to be revealed, for no matter how intense my sufferings are at the present time, that eternal glory is worth the wait.

PRAYER

Dear Lord Jesus,

You are my life, and I long for your return. When you come back to earth to take me to heaven, I will have a new body and mind and will appear with you in glory. Today, my body and mind are imperfect, and my burdens are incredibly heavy and seemingly never-ending. But your Word reminds me that these struggles are achieving for me an eternal glory that far outweighs all my problems. Thank you that my temporary depression, anxiety, and fears are preparing me for the unimaginable, unfathomable, and indescribable glory you have in store for me as a gift. Today I choose to eagerly anticipate the glory you will reveal to me, for I believe that the eternal glory is worth the wait. I pray this in Jesus' name, the one who is coming back to take me to heaven, amen.

MOVING FORWARD:

- Take out a piece of paper, and on the left side, write down a list of all your mental health troubles. On the right side, write down how these problems will change in heaven when

Christ returns. For example:

Anxiety about children/finances	*Complete peace*
Poor self-esteem	*Perfect and secure contentment*
Emotional pain	*Great joy*
Inability control my addictions	*Complete freedom*
Suicidal thoughts	*Abundant eternal life*

- Now add to your list.
- Across the page write, "All mine to be gained when Christ returns"

How much do you truly believe God when he says your present temporary troubles are achieving for you an eternal glory that far outweighs all your pain and illness?

SIXTY-NINE
FORGIVING WHEN IT HURTS

"Bear with each other and forgive one another if any of you has a grievance against someone. Forgive as the Lord forgave you."
— Colossians 3:13

Forgiveness is certainly not a simple concept to grasp, nor is it simple to do. If I do not remain upset at someone who accidentally steps on my feet on a busy street, does that mean I have forgiven him or her? If someone were to spread false rumors about me, and I do not hold any bitterness against that person, does *that* mean I have forgiven him or her? We are called to forgive all *grievances* we may have against each other. The term implies some degree of dissatisfaction, annoyance, or resentment that we may feel toward another person. If no one has been hurt or wounded, and if no one has committed any sin against anyone, then perhaps there is nothing to forgive in the first place. But what we *must* do is forgive as the Lord forgave us.

It is easy to think that we're good "forgivers" when little or no harm has been done to us, but when someone irritates, frustrates, angers, or hurts us in more significant ways, can we extend to them the gracious forgiveness of God? If only we could comprehend the true weight of our iniquity and wickedness in the eyes of the Lord, we would be better able to understand the indescribable and incomparable grace he has shown in forgiving us of all our sins. I don't think any of us can imagine how deeply we have angered God with our sins, but still, the Lord chose to lay his wrath on his only begotten Son so that we may find forgiveness in him and enjoy a brand-new relationship with our loving God.

Sometimes it may seem far too difficult to forgive those who have brought us deep, deep pain, but as we remember just how much we ourselves have been forgiven, we can trust that God will grant us the strength and ability to freely and fully forgive even our most "unforgivable" enemies.

PRAYER

Dear God,

I have sinned against and hurt you many times with my disobedient actions, inappropriate words, and poor attitude, yet you forgave me by laying my sins on Jesus who died for me on the cross. I accept your grace, mercy, and forgiveness, knowing that I do not deserve it. Now teach me how to extend the same grace, mercy, and forgiveness to all those who have hurt me in the past, those who are grieving me at present, and those who will upset me in the future. When I struggle to forgive others, please remind me of what a wretched a sinner I am and how you forgive me every time I sincerely repent before you. Help me never to use my mental health problems as an excuse not to forgive others. Remind me today whom I must forgive, and please give me the ability to do it fully and freely. I pray this in the forgiving name of Jesus, amen.

MOVING FORWARD:

- Write a list of your sins for which you have sought forgiveness from God. For each sin, remember that God has forgiven you. Also, write down the qualities God is transforming and developing in you. Remembering God's forgiveness can help you forgive others. Here are some examples to get you started:

A complaining attitude	→	*FORGIVEN*	→	*A grateful heart*
Being ungrateful	→	*FORGIVEN*	→	*Being thankful*
Not honoring parents	→	*FORGIVEN*	→	*Honoring parents*
Sexually impure thoughts	→	*FORGIVEN*	→	*Sexual purity*
A prideful attitude	→	*FORGIVEN*	→	*A humble heart*
Jealousy	→	*FORGIVEN*	→	*Thankfulness*
Seeking our own will	→	*FORGIVEN*	→	*Submitting to God's*
Unresolved anger	→	*FORGIVEN*	→	*Gentleness*

Who do you need to forgive while kneeling in prayer before God?

SEVENTY
I CAN'T

"Whatever you do, whether in word or deed, do it all in the name of the Lord Jesus, giving thanks to God the Father through him."

— Colossians 3:17

Over the past while, I have come to develop the habit of backing out of responsibilities and duties. My life feels like one big lie. I'd always been perceived to be a reliable and dependable person, but now I go out of my way to escape commitments, making excuses and fabricating stories to get myself out of responsibilities. Any feeling of "fatness," desperation, confusion, or hopelessness can trigger me to tell these lies. I will even avoid doing things I genuinely love and look forward to because of these thoughts and feelings. I tell people I am unable to come to this and that because I'm "sick." While I often do feel truly "sick," my excuse is only part of the reason I dodge responsibilities. Whatever happened to my dedication to people and things? I now feel so unwilling to commit myself to anyone or anything because I'm so afraid of breaking my commitments and continuing to lose people's trust.

Maybe I have forgotten that every little thing I do should be done for the glory of the Lord and *for him alone*. My life shouldn't be so much about what *I* myself want to do or feel like doing; it should be about me doing things that please him and bring honor and praise to him. God has given me different tasks to accomplish in this life, and even when I *feel* no motivation for doing these "missions," I must ask and trust that he will equip me with sufficient strength to do them. If out of nothing else but my love for and devotion to Christ, I must do *all* things with a deep thankfulness to God rather than with a sense of begrudging duty, remembering always that my commitment is first and foremost to my faithful and loving Lord.

PRAYER

Dear Lord,
Your Word teaches me to say all my words and do all my deeds in the name of the Lord Jesus. Your Word also teaches me to give thanks to you, God the Father, through Jesus. Help me to do this today and every day. I have become so unwilling to commit myself to anyone or anything because I am so afraid of breaking those commitments and losing people's trust. Thank you for reminding me again that I need to do all in the name of Jesus and for the glory of God. Help me commit myself to people and trust people as I learn to do things in Jesus' name and for your glory. As you give me different tasks to accomplish in life with other people, help me to trust you to equip me with sufficient strength to fulfill these duties in Jesus' name, always giving thanks to you, my Heavenly Father. I pray this in Jesus' name, for the glory of God, amen.

MOVING FORWARD:

- Every time you are asked to do a task, especially when you feel you are unable to do it because of your symptoms, say the following phrase several times: "I *will do* this deed in the name of my Lord Jesus, for the glory of God. Thank you, Lord, for helping me."

- As you are completing your task, say the following phrase: "God *is helping me finish* this task for the sake of my Lord Jesus, for his glory."
- After you complete your task, say the following phrase: "I *have done* this task in the name of my Lord Jesus, for the glory of God. Thank you, Lord, for helping me."
- Practice these phrases several times today.

Do you believe that the Scripture, "whatever you do," truly means everything you do? Why or why not? When is a time that doing something "for the glory of God" motivated you when you felt tired and weak?

SEVENTY-ONE
I WON'T BE SILENT

"Devote yourselves to prayer, being watchful and thankful."
— Colossians 4:2

Prayer changes things. Oh, my dear friends, how prayer truly does change things! Our situations may not *seem* to be different, nor may our difficulties disappear in their entirety, but nevertheless, *prayer changes things*. If the God we serve created us with purpose, then it would make little sense for him to ask us to pray continually if he didn't have the perfect reason for us to do so. I may not know the precise mechanisms by which the power of prayer is wielded, but of this I am certain: our Father is listening, and the Holy Spirit is the most accurate translator for us, turning our jumbled messes of thoughts into sweet-smelling incense flowing upwards to the throne of God.

There is no doubt that God hears every prayer we utter, and his heart must be moved when we bring our requests to him with all sincerity in our souls. Even our *human* hearts are moved and touched by honest, genuine, God-focused prayers. I think of Jesus, our Lord, who first came to step between our sinful, fallen selves and the perfect, holy Father, giving up his sinless life in order to establish for us our righteousness before God. This same Jesus, who now sits at the right hand of God, continues to intercede for us his servants, his followers, his children. What more motivation do we need?

We aren't called to merely offer up random prayers for random reasons at random times. We are called to *devote* ourselves to prayer, fully committing ourselves to this practice that causes mountains to move and lives to be restored. We may not necessarily see the desired fruits of our prayers immediately, but the encouragement to be faithful in prayer remains the same. Pray when you "feel like it," pray when you *don't* "feel like it." Pray when you think you need to, pray when you *don't* think you need to. Don't give up on prayer when you feel discouraged or doubtful, for it may be then when God gives you the opportunity to witness his timely responses to your requests. Thank him. Adore him. Watch for him. Whatever you do, don't stop praying. Just keep on. Keep on.

PRAYER

Dear Heavenly Father,

Help me to devote myself to prayer, being watchful and thankful. Teach me what it means to devote myself to prayer and pray continually. Show me what it means to be watchful, and please help me to be thankful. Convince me today that prayer truly changes things. Thank you, Father, for hearing all my prayers, and thank you, Jesus, for being my prayer advocate for every request I make. Thank you, Holy Spirit, for receiving all my prayers as sweet-smelling incense to the throne of the Father. Help me to be patient in waiting for your responses to my prayers, knowing that your answers are always perfect. I will choose to trust you fully as you respond to my prayers. My pain and trials should never be an excuse not to devote myself to prayer; they should be a reminder to pray continually and be watchful and thankful. I pray this in the name of the one who intercedes for me, Jesus, my prayer advocate, amen.

MOVING FORWARD:

- Look up the following words in a dictionary and get a better understanding of their meaning: devote, watchful, and continually. Now apply these definitions as you pray and seek the Lord today.

- Pick a day and *devote* yourself to several hours of *continuous* prayer. Be *watchful* as you see God answer your pleas and requests.

When was the last time you devoted yourself to prayer?

SEVENTY-TWO
AFRAID

"In spite of this, you did not trust in the LORD your God, who went ahead of you on your journey, in fire by night and in a cloud by day, to search out places for you to camp and to show you the way you should go."

— Deuteronomy 1:32-33

If only I could see God going ahead of me in a cloud in everything I do. Despite knowing that the Lord is with me in all I do and wherever I may go, it is easy to forget, feeling rather like I am left battling attacks from the enemy on my own. If only I could physically see the Lord staying right by me no matter what . . .

Lately, I have been feeling like I'm becoming more and more like a child. Not in the sense of becoming more "innocent" and "trusting"; rather, I see myself being scared of every little thing. I am overwhelmed by the smallest problems, afraid to venture just even a millimeter away from my sources of comfort, and needing someone to hold my hand through everything I do. I long so much to simply feel safe, to have some sort of security blanket I can bring with me everywhere and cling tightly to when even a slight feeling of fear arises in me. I am not certain why I am experiencing such insecurity, but what I do know is that my Lord, my ever-present help in time of trouble, has been going ahead of me all this time, paving my paths for me, fighting my enemies for me, and carrying me through every obstacle and roadblock that has been in my way. I am *not* alone, nor have I ever been left alone by God. How can I not trust him? How can I so quickly forget his faithfulness, providence, and unceasing watch and care over my life?

It is not easy to always feel the presence of God when the world seems comfortless and unkind, but I must believe and remember that *he is with me*. What can harm me? What can create unconquerable fear and anxiety in me? Nothing, for God is with me. Always.

PRAYER

Dear Lord,

You see my anxiety and fear of what lies ahead of me. I cannot see in the future, but you can. You promise to go ahead of me in my healing, and in the care of all of my spiritual and physical needs. You care for every flower, every sparrow, and also every need I have. You are my Lord, my comforter, and my ever-present help in times of trouble. You promise to be with me and to go before me daily. Please help me to trust you, especially when I am afraid and overwhelmed by the smallest of problems. Please remind me daily of your faithfulness, providence and unceasing watch and care over my life. I am your child and you love me dearly. Please take away my anxiety and fear of what lies ahead, for you are with me always. In the faithful name of Jesus, my light and my shield, amen.

MOVING FORWARD:

- Write down three important events you are anticipating in the next few months and years. This could be an appointment with a doctor, a medical test, surgery, starting a new medication, graduation, a holiday, the purchase of an important item, etc. Next to each event, write down the things you are worried about and the things you cannot control. Now pray and ask the Lord to take care of every detail in each of those events. Then, in large letters, write the words, "My Heavenly Father goes before me and will help me."

- Repeat this every time you anticipate a future event that causes you to be anxious or afraid.

How does God's faithfulness to you in the past help you trust him for the care of your future health and well-being?

SEVENTY-THREE
HOLDING NOTHING BACK

"What other nation is so great as to have their gods near them the way the LORD our God is near us whenever we pray to him."

— Deuteronomy 4:7

There is none like our God. There never has been, and there never will be, another like him. How incredible and absolutely baffling it is to think that the God of creation, the God of the universe, the everlasting God, this amazing God and Sustainer of all things, is near us whenever we pray to him. And we, who are like mere *dust*, are the precious objects of his affections and tender care. How incomprehensible, yet how beautiful and true.

It isn't *only* the greatness of God that makes him altogether glorious, but the fact that such a magnificent God would stoop so low to human level out of his deep love and compassion for us is just astonishing; it's extraordinary. What tremendous comfort it should bring us to know that we have this awesome

God on our side, taking care of every detail of our lives. He who wipes away the tears of a child who has lost her favorite toy is the same God who replaces storm clouds with rainbows and darkness with light. Why then do I neglect to bring before him my every joy, my every sorrow, my every praise, my every request?

I can stop merely reciting to God in prayer carefully phrased words I think he would like to hear, for he has given us the amazing privilege of pouring out our deepest concerns and needs to him. The Lord desires to hear the expressions of our hearts, so he comes near to us when we draw near to him. He doesn't stand far away with his arms crossed, ready to catch our every grammatical error and mistake; he sees the hidden longings of our souls and comes close to touch our wounds with his nail-scarred hands. We must treasure this beautiful relationship we have with our great God, being assured that when we come to him in reverence, awe, and genuine worship, we will find in him complete and utter satisfaction that we won't ever find elsewhere.

PRAYER

Dear God,

Thank you for being close to me when I pray to you. You are an awesome God who takes care of every detail of my life. My prayers are important to you when it comes to my needs and the desires of my heart. Why then am I so reluctant to share with you all my sorrows, my fears, my sins, my disappointments, my pains, my heart, and my soul? Help me to stop reciting prayers that don't come from my heart; I want to pour out my deep pain and struggles. I believe that you can see the hidden longings of my heart and are longing to pour out your grace and mercy on me, your child. Help me come to you in genuine worship as I pray, and help me find complete and utter satisfaction in my relationship with you. I pray these things in the name of my loving Jesus, the hearer and answerer of my prayers, amen.

MOVING FORWARD:

- Kneel down and pray right now. As you pray, try not to worry about the words, but rather, concentrate on sharing with God all of your *emotions*. Include your pain, joys, fears, frustrations, anger, hurts, and disappointments. Remind yourself of the following verses:

- John 4:24: "God is spirit, and his worshippers must worship in spirit and truth
- Romans 8:26-27: "Likewise the Spirit helps us in our weakness. For we do not know what to pray for as we ought, but the Spirit himself intercedes for us with groanings too deep for words. And he who searches hearts knows what is the mind of the Spirit, because the Spirit intercedes for the saints according to the will of God" (ESV).

When you pray, what do you concentrate more on: your words, your emotions, your needs, or your worship? How can you practice pouring all these things out to the Lord in your prayers?

SEVENTY-FOUR
PLEASE DON'T LET ME FORGET

"Be careful that you do not forget the LORD."

— Deuteronomy 6:12

Do not forget the Lord. Don't forget that he is there to gather your tears and bind your wounds when all seems to go against you. Don't forget him when your days are bright, and you feel there to be "little need" to run to the Lord for help. Don't forget that he is ready to fill you with great joy when the mundane routines of life seem so dull and dry that you begin to lose all motivation and passion to work diligently for the Lord. Do not forget the Lord.

There have been many times when I had quickly skimmed over this verse thinking I didn't need the reminder, but I surprise myself with how easily and quickly I sometimes let God "slip" to the back of my mind. Too many times, he isn't the first one I turn to for comfort and direction. Too many times, I thank people before I thank him. Too many times, I spill out my troubles and concerns to other people before pouring out my deepest needs to him. It seems counterintuitive that our hearts neglect the *greatest One of all* and that we choose to concern ourselves with the lesser things of life, but this is indeed a very real danger. And doesn't that happen in so many other areas of our lives as well? It is too hard to see the "big picture" things in life, so instead, we magnify the trivial and insignificant.

Whatever situation or circumstance we might be facing, we must remember to turn our hearts and souls toward the Lord, not only because then we can view things as they truly are, but also so that we can receive from him the grace and strength we need to overcome every struggle and trial.

PRAYER

Dear God,

Please forgive me for frequently forgetting you. I often turn to my own resources, wisdom, and knowledge before turning to you for help. I frequently seek the encouragement of other people before turning to you for strength and peace. I don't want to forget you, but I often do. Please help me to thank you before thanking people and to talk to you about every situation before talking to people. I want you, my God, my Lord, and my Counselor, to be my closest companion, advisor, and friend. During times of deep depression, significant anxiety, and other severe mental health problems, help me to seek you first. During times of good mental health, joy, and peace, please remind me to thank you first and look to you first. Help me to love you, my Savior, more than anyone else. I pray this in the name of my heavenly counselor, Jesus, amen.

MOVING FORWARD:

- Write down three to five things that took place in the last month. Now ask yourself if you talked to God about any of them. For example:

- You had an appointment with a medical provider. Did you ask the Lord for wisdom, guidance, patience, and peace regarding that appointment?
- You visited a friend. Did you invite the Holy Spirit to your conversation and meal?
- You attended a social gathering. Was prayer part of the event, and did Jesus come up in any conversation?

Do you think you could remember God every hour? What kind of prompt or reminder would you need?

SEVENTY-FIVE
IDOLS BE GONE

"This is what you are to do to them: Break down their altars, smash their sacred stones, cut down their Asherah poles and burn their idols in the fire. For you are a people holy to the LORD your God. The LORD your God has chosen you out of all the peoples on the face of the earth to be his people, his treasured possession."

— Deuteronomy 7:5-6

As I was listening to a pastor speak on the issue of addiction, I was reminded of how addictions can be a manifestation of underlying hearts of idolatry. This realization can help us change not only our behaviors, but also our hearts. A question I think we all need to ask ourselves is: What idols have I chosen to worship before God? The idol of appearance? The idol of acceptance? The idol of success? What or whom have I chosen to place above, or take the place of, the one and only true God?

I imagine it can be easy to forget that our idols are, in fact, idols because their false promises and deceptive lies can seem so convincing. Do we turn to one or several of our idols to find our identity, security, relief, and comfort, or do we depend wholly on our Lord to provide us with all these and more? Do we seek absolute satisfaction in God, or do we search for elusive fulfillment from our idols? When we wake up in the morning, is our first thought one of gratitude and praise to God, or do we start coming up with ways to "worship" our idols that day?

I understand how addictive the drawing power of idols are, yet none of them deserve our worship. The only one we must give our hearts and lives to is God. When we surrender to anything or anyone else, we only become consumed, overwhelmed, overpowered, and ultimately, defeated. The only life-giving choice we can make is to break our idols, smashing any behavior and means by which we give ourselves to them. We must destroy all that hinders us from worshiping the one true God; we truly must seize our idols and burn them in fire. We are the people of God, and thus, to him rightly belong our thoughts, hearts, devotion, faith, reliance, our *lives.*

The promises of idols will always be empty ones, but the promises of God will eternally be true and sure. Our God who created us intimately knows and will meet our every need. We need not, and *must not,* seek our satisfaction and contentment elsewhere. "Therefore, my dear friends, flee from idolatry" (1 Corinthians 10:14). Indeed, we must run from idolatry and instead run straight into the arms of God as fast as we can, for there, at last, our hunger and thirsts will be quenched, and we will be satisfied in ways beyond our highest expectations.

PRAYER

Dear Lord,

What are my idols today? Who and what am I worshiping these days? Is it the idol of appearance, or acceptance, or success? Am I seeking to gain fulfillment and joy through my idols, through you, or through both? Do I search for happiness in people and in earthly possessions rather than in you alone? Please forgive me, for I have sinned. As I struggle with my eating disorder or addictions, help me to destroy these idols and worship you alone. Teach me to not just ignore idols, but to flee from them. Today you have taught me that I am a person holy to you, Lord God. You have chosen me to be your child, your treasured possession. Now please help me to break all the ways in which I worship idols, smashing any behavior and means by which I give myself to them. In the name of the only true God, Jesus, amen.

MOVING FORWARD:

- Take out a piece of paper and list your idols. If you are not sure you have any, consider the following in your personal life: appearance, acceptance, certain people involved in your health care, T.V. personalities, sports figures, your children, spouse, best friend, and the pursuit of happiness. What do you crave more than God? Now list ways to destroy these idols by specific changes in your behaviour. Seek advice from trained professionals, such as pastors, counselors, and Christian doctors.

What does it mean to flee from idols? What does that look like in your everyday life?

SEVENTY-SIX
THE CHOICE IS MINE

"See, I set before you today life and prosperity, death and destruction."

— Deuteronomy 30:15

There are always two paths set before us, aren't there? One that leads us to the prosperous life God desires for us, and the other that leads to a future of darkness and destruction that he died to rescue us from. Sometimes it seems like there are a great number of options that lie between the "good" and the "bad," but I think that every choice we make can only be either pleasing to the Lord or not. No small choice of ours is mundane in the eyes of him who cares about every minute detail of our lives, and whether we choose to obey him or disobey him matters greatly to our Father in heaven.

People have told me that I always have the ability to choose how to feel and how not to feel. I disagree because if I could choose not to feel hopeless, unloved, lonely, desperate, scared, frightened, or unsure, I would. But I can't. At least, I don't know how. But while I don't know how much choice and control we have over our feelings, I do not deny that we *can* often choose our *responses* to those feelings. In my most depressing times, I can choose to seek, claim, and dwell in the everlasting joy of God. In my angriest moments, I can choose to pray for a forgiving and gracious heart. The feelings themselves may not change spontaneously, but by turning to the Lord rather than reacting as I wish, I can receive the delight that flows from living in obedience to my King. "Choose life and not death!" (2 Kings 18:32). Our very Lord desires for us to choose *life* and all the things that this choice encompasses. I think we would do well to echo these words spoken long ago, living in accordance to them regardless of how difficult and inconvenient it may sometimes seem.

PRAYER

Dear Heavenly Father,

Thank you for setting before me life and not death, prosperity and not destruction. Thank you for dying on the cross in my place to rescue me from eternal separation from you. I have not chosen to suffer from my mental disorder, and I am often unable to control the thoughts and feelings of hopelessness, loneliness, desperation, and fear that frequently come upon me. Please help me to give helpful response to those thoughts and feelings. I plead that today I will make every choice pleasing to you. In my most depressing times, help me to choose to seek, claim, and dwell in the everlasting joy of knowing you as my best friend. In my angriest moments, remind me to choose to pray for a forgiving and gracious heart. Help me to always turn to you, rather than react in harmful ways to my feelings. Help me to live in obedience to you, my King, as I choose life and prosperity, rather than death and destruction. I pray these things in the name of Jesus, the giver of life, amen.

MOVING FORWARD:

- Go for a walk through a safe and familiar part of your city to try an exercise highlighting the importance of making sound choices. Make a conscious decision of where you would like to get to. Begin your journey, and as you walk up to each intersection, flip a coin. If the coin lands on heads, turn right, and if it lands on tails, turn left. After thirty minutes of walking, see where your choices have taken you. You will likely be far from your desired, chosen destination. Then make a conscious decision to head home. As you walk up to each intersection, make a choice as to which way to turn, based on what you know is the correct destination. If you make the correct choices, you should reach your home. Wrong choices will get you lost, whereas correct choices will bring you to your desired destination.

- In your daily life, strive to intentionally seek the Lord as you make your decisions, relying on God's wisdom rather than your own, particularly when you are experiencing strong and intense emotions.

What are you using as the roadmap for your choices? What can help you follow the Bible, God's roadmap?

SEVENTY-SEVEN
CAN'T STAND ALONE

"And let us consider how we may spur one another on toward love and good deeds."

— Hebrews 10:24

We cannot go "solo" through life. It doesn't work. Believe me. I've been trying to do precisely that, and it doesn't work. If we view each of our lives as one burning candle, it is easy to imagine how vulnerable we are if we stand alone. It wouldn't take much for our flame to quickly dim, flicker, and die, no matter how "long lasting" we might have been designed to be. A strong wind might do it, a slight movement, even a change of location. It is quite easy to very neatly and easily snuff out our flame.

But what if we do not stand alone, but rather are placed in a community of fellow defenseless candles? Sure, our flames might still waver with waves of doubts and uncertainties, but we can be more easily revived and restored by a neighboring flame that might be burning stronger and more confidently than we are at the time.

I have been so drawn to solitude for such a long time that I am unsure as to whether or not I can ever fully adjust to "social life" again. I don't know if I feel ready to give up the safety that can be found in being alone, nor do I feel prepared to truly offer my life for the sake of others who I have been called to fellowship with. But can I remember that in order for other believers and me to be effective in our work for the Lord, we must constantly give and receive encouragement from our family in Christ? Discouragement and criticisms come often enough from the devil, and I think God has placed us in the body of Christ so that we can spur each other onwards, cheering for one another when successes come and lifting each other up when we fail and lose sight of our hope. "Let us not give up meeting together, as some are in the habit of doing, but let us encourage one another—and all the more as you see the Day approaching" (Hebrews 10:25).

PRAYER

Dear Heavenly Father,

I have often tried to get through life going "solo." I have been drawn to solitude for such a long time, and I am afraid to give up the safety that I find in being alone. I realize, though, that this is not your will for my life. Please forgive me. I don't feel prepared to truly offer my life for the sake of others who you have called me to fellowship with. Teach me how I can daily give and receive encouragement from my church family. Help me to do away with discouragement and criticism and replace it with words and actions that cheer other Christians on to love and good deeds. Give me the strength and health to meet regularly with the family of God for worship, prayer, the study of your Word, and to do good works. Remind me always that this is for my benefit and your glory. I pray these things in the name of Jesus, the One whom I delight in fellowshipping with daily, amen.

MOVING FORWARD:

- Write down two to three ways someone has encouraged you to either love other Christians more or to do good deeds.

- Choose one of them and make a decision to do the same in order to help someone else.
- If you can't think of one, consider some of the following examples:
    - Pray with someone over the phone.
    - Send an encouraging email.
    - Go and visit someone who has been discouraged or ill and share an encouraging word.

      Especially consider those who have been unable to attend church for reasons of problems with their mental or physical health.

What are some tangible ways for you to encourage others? How do you feel about giving someone an encouraging book, such as this one?

SEVENTY-EIGHT
LOUDNESS OF MY FAITH

"By faith the walls of Jericho fell, after the army had marched around them for seven days."

— Hebrews 11:30

Wow. Those people must have marched with very heavy steps, or their trumpets must have been quite loudly sounded, or their shouts must have been wall-shatteringly thunderous. But maybe not. I think that even if they all had broken ankles, or blown muted trumpets, or all came down with a serious case of strep throat so that they were unable to holler, the walls would still have come down as long as they obeyed. Those walls fell because of *faith*—the people's faith that God would do as he promised. They needed only to trust and be obedient.

Wouldn't it be so much easier if our struggles could be overcome by following some "formula" of sorts? If not marching around a city for a few days, then maybe something that resembles dipping ourselves several times in a river (2 Kings 5)? But am I not still missing the heart of what God is trying to teach us? These actions didn't "work" because the people had faith in the power of what was *being done*; they worked because the people relied on *God* with whom nothing is impossible. The woman who reached for Jesus probably realized that the simple act of touching *a* cloak wouldn't make a difference to her health, but the cloak she touched was the Lord's, and her faith that *he* could heal her ultimately led to healing indeed (Matthew 9:20-22; Mark 5:25-34; Luke 8:43-48). The blind men who answered the simple question regarding their belief in Jesus' power likely did not think their verbal response itself would affect whether or not their sight would be restored, but the Lord healed them according to their profession of faith (Matthew 9:27-31).

The Lord can bring about healing in numerous ways—some that seem "logical" and some that may be just unthinkable. In the end, it is our *faith* that pleases him and what he desires to see manifested in us. May we truly hear and understand what Jesus meant when he said, "Your faith has healed you" (Matthew 9:22).

PRAYER

Dear God,

Just as the Israelites believed the walls of Jericho would fall as they obeyed you, I also believe that you can heal me as I obey you. They had to obey you exactly as instructed, and I desire to obey you exactly as you instruct me. Please show me clearly what I need to do in order to be healed, and give me the strength and courage to obey. Although my faith is small, it is present and real, and it is in you. My ultimate faith and trust is in you; it is not in doctors, medications, therapies, rehabilitation programs, or hospitals, though all of these can be important tools you use for my healing. Just as the Israelites had to walk and blow trumpets, I will follow through on your instructions for my healing. I plead to you for a spontaneous healing, but I am willing to accept your plan of healing even if it is over seven days, seven months, seven years, or my lifetime. I pray this by faith, in the name of Jesus, the One who gives me faith, amen.

MOVING FORWARD:

- Find a close Christian friend or family member to partner with you in the following activity:

- Consider spending a day in prayer, fasting, and reading the Bible, asking God to show you his plan of healing for your mental health problems.
- Discuss this plan with your pastor, Christian doctor, and/or Christian counselor.
- You may want to use this devotional book as a resource for your healing plan.
- Ask God to help you believe and obey his plan for your healing.

In what ways do you need healing right now? How much do you truly believe that God is your ultimate healer?

SEVENTY-NINE
WHAT TIME IS IT?

"There is a time for everything, and a season for every activity under heaven."
— Ecclesiastes 3:1

I once met a child who *always* wanted to know the time. He repeatedly asked the question, "What time is it?" every few minutes. Whatever anxiety or reason made him preoccupied with the progress of the minute hand, I feel the urge to ask myself this question: *What time is it in my life*? What are the things that are meant for me to do in this season? What must I begin? What must I end? What must I put on hold? Especially for someone like me who wants to do *everything*, *now*, this may be an especially important question to consider.

In a somewhat bittersweet way, I am learning that it can be okay to let go of old friends and welcome new ones. While the painful feelings of loss and loneliness may inevitably arise, there is no need to be hopeless and afraid. There is a time for everything—a time to start a friendship, a time to end one, and a time to rebuild. Perhaps the time has come for me to learn the painful lessons that are found in weakening and failing relationships. This is not for me to use as an excuse to avoid mending and restoring broken relationships as far as it is possible with me, but I think it is a reminder to recognize the purpose, and even beauty, that God can bring out of the darkest times in our lives. And who knows, maybe somewhere down the road, the time to rebuild lost friendships will dawn. For now, I must trust that the God of all the seasons in my life will provide me with the strength and courage to walk through *this* very season, filling me with sure hope and confidence that he will bring me safely through.

PRAYER

Dear God,

What time is it in my life? What are the things I need to do in this season? What must I begin, and what must I end? What must I put on hold? I am often anxious and impatient and want things "now." Please forgive me. You are taking me through this season of depression and anxiety. Please help me understand that you have a good purpose even in this time of my life, and help me recognize the beauty that you can bring out of the darkness. I pray that you help me honestly evaluate my friendships from your perspective. Which ones are not your will and need to be ended? Which friendships need to be restored? Please provide me with some new friends who you will use to bless, shape, sharpen, and encourage me in this painful season. I ask for you to help me trust you for strength, courage, hope, and confidence, as you bring me through this season. I pray these things in the name of Jesus, my closest friend, amen.

MOVING FORWARD:

- Make a list of all your friends. Divide them into two groups. In the first group, place those who are a positive influence in your life. In the second group, write down any who may be a negative or destructive influence in your life. Now ask the Lord to help you confirm your friendships with the first group and possibly end some of the relationships in the second group. Ask God for strength, courage, hope, and confidence to put this plan into action. You may need the help of a close friend such as your spouse, parent, or pastor.

- If you are struggling to find supportive friends, ask the Lord to bring loving Christ followers into your life who can strengthen and encourage you in your recovery and in your pursuit of God.

When was the last time you thoughtfully evaluated your friendships from God's point of view?

EIGHTY
IN YOUR TIME, NOT MINE

"He has made everything beautiful in its time. He has also set eternity in the hearts of men; yet they cannot fathom what God has done from beginning to end."

— Ecclesiastes 3:11

Everything will be beautiful one day. The beauty that has been marred by sin will one day be restored to its fullness and splendor. I don't know about you, but I can't wait for that to happen. And this makes sense because the imperfect, tainted beauty of this world cannot possibly satisfy the deepest longings of our hearts. We were created for eternity; thus, like fish out of water, we cannot be content for long with that which is fleeting and temporal. We are all searching for something more—something unchangingly glorious, something eternally beautiful. We are all seeking for God to fulfill all that our hearts and souls crave and desire.

It is needless to say that I am quite dissatisfied and

displeased with certain aspects of myself—my appearance, my thoughts, my character, my inabilities . . . But can I not accept that the Lord is well on his way in scraping off all the imperfect marks and blotches from my fallen self, restoring me to the perfect piece of creation he had so intricately and thoughtfully designed before the beginning of time? If I turn my eyes to my Lord, I will find that though we may be broken, we can also be beautiful because our most beautiful God has come to dwell in our hearts and be King over our very lives. Let's not focus on the imperfections; rather, we must rest our eyes on our perfect God, inviting him to shine forth his beauty through us.

Everything has been made beautiful, so trust that one day we will be able to fully understand and taste for ourselves what beauty is truly like.

PRAYER

Dear God,

You truly have made everything beautiful in its time. It is particularly difficult for me currently to fathom what you have done from beginning to end. You have created me for eternity, and yet I only see the present, forgetting what lies ahead in your perfect plan to make me beautiful. Because of my eating disorder and other conditions, I really struggle to like and accept my appearance, my thoughts, my character, and my inabilities. Please help me to see myself as I will one day become, as you restore me to the perfect piece of creation you so intricately and thoughtfully designed before the beginning of time. Although I am broken, in your eyes I am also beautiful. No illness or struggle can ever change that fact. Help me to not focus on my imperfections, but rather to rest my eyes on you, my creator. I invite you to shine forth your beauty through me. I pray this in the beautiful name of Jesus, the restorer of my soul, amen.

MOVING FORWARD:

- Take out a piece of paper, and on the left side of the page, write out at least five things you don't like about yourself or wish are different. Examples may be your weight, facial appearance, aspects of your character, etc. Now draw an arrow from the left side of the page to the right. On the arrow, write, "God will make everything beautiful in its time." On the right side of the page, write, "Done." Remind yourself frequently that God never fails. His plan for and task of making you beautiful and restoring you from brokenness to wholeness will never fail. For example:

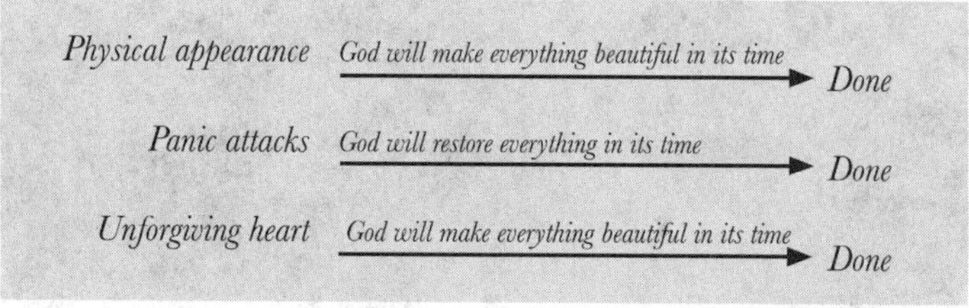

- Pray and ask God to help you fully understand and taste what beauty is truly like.

Do you believe that God cannot fail at the task of making you beautiful in his perfect time? What would help you truly believe that he will succeed?

EIGHTY-ONE
A POOR REFLECTION

"Now we see only a reflection as in a mirror; then we shall see face to face."
— 1 Corinthians 13:12a

It truly is rather strange how quickly my perceptions of people's appearances change. I might perceive a person as being of "normal weight" one day, and the very next day, I might see the same person as being extremely thin. Needless to say, this intensifies my feelings of distress and anxiety. Although I know in my mind that it is highly unlikely for anyone's weight to fluctuate so dramatically in the span of a day, somehow I cannot convince my eyes to see the skewed nature of what I perceive as reality.

As I think of my distorted perceptions of weight, I am left wondering just how skewed my perceptions are of other things in my life. When I encounter problems that seem frighteningly gigantic, am I merely magnifying them all in my mind? I must realize that even the strongest-powered glasses cannot correct the imperfect vision I use to view the world. There are so many factors that influence the things I see and the ways I see these things, and I must remember that until the day when all will be made right again, my perceptions will always be at least slightly distorted and, perhaps, slightly tainted.

Do I think I have "good" knowledge of the Lord right now? If so, then I must be careful not to forget that, at the present, what I see is but a poor reflection. There are still treasures untold and mysteries unrevealed. Let me simply cherish the knowledge I have been blessed with, trusting that although my understanding is incomplete, the Lord has given me his Spirit to guide me into all truth, making known to me the precious and secret things of God, and allowing me to grow in greater and greater maturity in him daily.

PRAYER

Dear God,

Thank you for giving me your Holy Spirit, which allows me to see your great eternal truths from your perspective. When I begin to look at my problems with my earthly eyes, I often become discouraged because I fail to see them from your perspective. Please forgive me. Help me now to see my problems and my illness as you see them and to understand the great work you are doing in my life, for your glory. For those things I may never see and understand clearly in this life on earth, help me trust in you. I look forward to the day when I shall see you face-to-face, for at that time, you will help me understand all things more clearly. In the name of Jesus, who created me in his image, amen.

MOVING FORWARD:

- Pull out some old photographs from your own childhood and over the years of your life. Lay them out in chronological order and ask yourself how you viewed yourself and the world at each of those stages in your life. Then remind yourself that you are God's child, and he is not finished with you yet. He has seen you through each moment on your life, and his loving view of you will remain constant throughout all of eternity.

When you look into the mirror at yourself, what thoughts do you have about how God, your loving creator, views your physical appearance?

EIGHTY-TWO
BETTER TOGETHER

"Two are better than one,
because they have a good return
for their labor:
If one falls down,
his friend can help him up.
But pity the man who falls
and has no one to help him up!"
— Ecclesiastes 4:9-10

We are called to live at peace with all people as long as it is possible for us, so why do I feel as if I don't even care if I upset my friends anymore? If they leave me, fine. If they hate me, fine. I feel so little motivation to even put in the effort to make things right with them. I allow misunderstandings to stew, I let misinterpretations remain convincing and falsely real . . . I feel like I just don't care. But friends are a good thing. No, friends are more than good. They are vital people we need in our lives. For if we fall (and who does not fall?) and are without a friend, we are left with no one to help or support us—we are indeed to be pitied.

You know, the concept of friendship must have been, and is, very close to the heart of Jesus. And if this is the case, how can we not treasure the people he has placed by our sides? "You are my friends if you do what I command. I no longer call you servants, because a servant does not know his master's business. Instead, I have called you friends, for everything that I learned from my Father I have made known to you" (John 15:14-15).

If *human* friends are ones we cannot go without, how much more fervently must we nurture the greatest friendship we can ever develop—an intimate relationship with our Savior? Two people are better than one, and a person with friends is better than one without, but who can possibly be more blessed than a person who is a beloved friend of God? God himself has come to earth to lay down his life for us, being the best, most trustworthy friend we can ever imagine. Let us model our friendships after that perfect one initiated by God. Let us love each other, help each other, and point each other to our beautiful Savior.

PRAYER

Dear Heavenly Father,

You have given me some very good friends, for whom I thank you. Help me to be a good friend to each of them, serving and loving them faithfully with your love. Help me restore my broken friendships and love each of my friends with unconditional love. My spouse is also my friend. You gave me my spouse as a special gift, for the rest of my life. Forgive me for the way I have sometimes dealt with my friends, including my spouse. The greatest friend you gave me is Jesus. He is my friend for all of eternity. He will never leave me or forsake me, never disappoint me, never gossip about me, never give up on me, and never lie to me. Thank you, Jesus, for calling me your friend. You have revealed to me everything you have learned from the Father. I want to renew my friendship with you today. In the precious name of my God and perfect friend, Jesus, amen.

MOVING FORWARD:

- Write down a list of your four closest friends. Place them in order from your closest friend at the top to the fourth closest friend at the bottom. Now ask yourself the following questions:

- Where is Jesus on that list?
- If you have a spouse, where is he or she on that list?
- Do I love each of these friends unconditionally with godly love?
- When my human friends fall, am I there to pick them up?
- In what ways can I encourage and bless these friends this week?

How important is it for Jesus to be your best friend? If you feel that Jesus is your best friend, do your actions, words, and attitude portray that?

EIGHTY-THREE
ANGER IGNITED

"Do not be quickly provoked in
your spirit, for anger resides in the lap of fools."
— Ecclesiastes 7:9

Anger often comes without warning, doesn't it? It can be the most "natural" and instinctive way for us to react in response to provocation or unjust treatment. In fact, I sometimes convince myself that I am entitled to be angry at someone when I feel that I have been wronged or otherwise offended. Sometimes I almost force myself to *be* angry at people, feeling like I must act cold and uncharacteristically "polite" and distant in order to show others how much I disapprove of what they have done, and to convey to them the magnitude of the hurt they have caused me. As much as I am reluctant to say this, there can be a certain degree of satisfaction in knowing that your displeasure is being communicated to another. After all, what better way for people to understand the pain they have caused other than to personally experience it themselves? How else can they truly know the hurt I am going through unless they feel the same thing?

Oh, but how void of love and forgiveness this all is! Whatever happened to loving my enemies and turning the other cheek for them to strike? What about forgiving others over and over again? The command is to "[d]o to others as you would have them do to you" (Luke 6:31), not do to others as they *have done* to you. This kind of anger that leads to resentment and desire for revenge is contrary to the righteous life God has called us to. "Get rid of all bitterness, rage and anger, brawling and slander, along with every form of malice" (Ephesians 4:31). We must treat one another with love, acceptance, and compassion. There is no avoiding the fact that we will all upset and disappoint each other as we share and navigate life together, but we must "love each other deeply, because love covers over a multitude of sins" (1 Peter 4:8). How I need God to calm my spirit in times when I feel like I have been taken advantage of and mistreated. I often know the ways in which I "should" act, but it is much more difficult to carry these things out. May I rely on the power of God to help me always respond with love and grace to those who harm or seek to harm me, choosing to bless rather than insult (1 Peter 3:9), living in peace with my brothers and sisters (Romans 12:18), and striving to do good for one another (1 Thessalonians 5:15).

PRAYER

Dear God,

I am often provoked quickly to anger. Although anger in and of itself is not a sin, in my anger, I often say and do things that are hurtful to others and to you. Please forgive me for my sins that are done in anger. Help me to be angry at the appropriate time, in the appropriate situation, with the appropriate attitude. Teach me to manage my anger in a way that brings benefit to your kingdom and glory to your name. Show me how to get rid of all bitterness, rage, anger, brawling, and slander, along with every form of malice. None of these come from love, acceptance, or compassion. Give me an extra measure of your grace and mercy today so that I can forgive and love others deeply, knowing that your love that flows through me covers a multitude of sins. I pray these things in the loving, patient, and forgiving name of Jesus, amen.

MOVING FORWARD:

- Over the next week, evaluate your episodes of anger by answering the following questions:
    - Why am I angry? Is it due to my own unresolved emotional pain, depression, fear, loneliness, or unresolved need to forgive others for wrongs done to me?
    - Could I have responded in a different way?
    - Am I capable of controlling my anger, or does my anger control me?
    - Do I need to repent of my thoughts and actions that were done in anger?

In what ways do you struggle with controlling your anger? What behaviors manifest themselves when you are angry?

EIGHTY-FOUR
PLEASE FREE ME

"God created mankind upright, but men have gone in search of many schemes."

— Ecclesiastes 7:29

I have come to realize how little resistance I put up against my many temptations to sin. How slow I am to put on the full armor of God to fight and ward off the vicious attacks of Satan! I have also come to realize, though, a rather frightening thing. Even if the devil were to leave me alone and spare me from his active pursuit, I would likely still seek out opportunities to sin and thus continue to break the commands of God. How can this be? My deepest desire is to live in complete obedience to God, so why would I knowingly and purposely engage in the very things that contradict his will for my life?

The devil works in such conniving, manipulative ways, and the pull and power of sin is so strong and unrelenting. Yet how blessed are we, for we are controlled not by our sinful nature but by the Spirit of God who lives within us. The God who created us righteous, who made us upright, is the same God who sees our appalling wickedness but chose to rescue us from our bondage to sin. "We all, like sheep, have gone astray, each of us has turned to his own way; and the LORD has laid on him the iniquity of us all" (Isaiah 53:6). In our sinfulness, we have chosen to turn away from the holiness of God, but yet, we can be filled with hope in the power of our risen Savior. We do not have to give in to the deceptive allure of sin, but we can be empowered by the Spirit to seek the treasures of God rather than the illusory pleasures of sin. Let's make it our aim to pursue the righteousness of God, striving to become more and more like the pure children he first created us to be.

PRAYER

Dear God,

I am your adopted child, filled with your Holy Spirit, yet I live in my sinful body that is daily tempted to turn away from your holiness. My deepest desire is to live in complete obedience to you, yet I keep breaking your commandments. Please forgive me for frequently going astray. You have provided me with the full armor of God, the Holy Spirit who resides in me, the Word of God that guides me, and your daily grace and mercy, which always provides me with an escape from all temptations. Help me not to give in to the deceptive allure of sin, especially when I am struggling with my addictions and other difficulties. Help me to overcome my addictions and sinful behavior by pursuing your righteousness. I repent of my sinful actions, and I plead for an extra measure of your grace and mercy to overcome each temptation today. Thank you that despite my appalling sinfulness, you have chosen to forgive me, love me, save me, cleanse me, and rescue me from the bondage of my sin and addictions. I pray these things in the saving name of Jesus, my deliverer, amen.

MOVING FORWARD:

- If you have any addictions or engage in

harmful patterns of behavior, acknowledge them before God today by confessing to him in prayer. These could include drugs, alcohol, pornography, television, self-injury, excessive work, greed, etc.

- Repent quickly before God every time you fall into these patterns and sin. He is quick to show mercy and slow to anger.
- Find a trustworthy friend who would be willing to pray with you every time you are tempted by your addictions. Call them and pray with them when the temptation comes.
- If you know someone who suffers from an addiction, support them by praying with them whenever they are tempted.

What jumps out to you about the truth that God's grace, mercy, and forgiveness to his children is everlasting, no matter how many times we sin? Does this truth make you want to rely on God's grace and stand firm when you are tempted to sin?

EIGHTY-FIVE
IN NEED OF STRENGTH

"Whatever your hand finds to do, do it with all your might, for in the realm of the dead, where you are going, there is neither working nor planning nor knowledge nor wisdom."

— Ecclesiastes 9:10

I never used to have a problem being motivated and working hard. I suppose I didn't realize just how precious the gift of self-discipline really is. It isn't that I have no desire to accomplish *anything* anymore—quite the contrary. There are so *many* things I would love to achieve and do—I simply have tremendous difficulty following through with and working toward these goals. God has placed in my heart the urgency and zeal to serve him and carry out the works of his kingdom, but because of all that is keeping me back from moving boldly forward, I feel like I am wasting my time, his gifts, and this life.

Jesus said, "As long as it is day, we must do the work of him who sent me. Night is coming, when no one can work" (John 9:4). There is little question that my mental health challenges are making it especially difficult to do the work I so desire to accomplish for the Lord. The pull to give up and quit can seem so powerful and controlling. But no, regardless of how dark and hopeless my life may seem, the Lord will not cease to be my shining light, determining the steps I take and directing me along the path I should travel. I can only pray that God will continue to fuel in my heart this flame of passion for him so that I will be strengthened and encouraged every moment to walk in obedience to him and be a faithful worker of God. "For we are God's handiwork, created in Christ Jesus to do good works, which God prepared in advance for us to do" (Ephesians 2:10).

PRAYER

Dear God,

You have given me life to live for your glory. Every day is a gift from you so that I can do the work you have prepared for me. I am your workmanship, created in Christ Jesus to do good works. Please forgive me for all of the times I have not been diligent in carrying out the work you have intended for me. Regardless of how dark and hopeless life may seem, please be my shining light, determining the steps I take, and directing me along the path I should go. I ask that you would fuel in my heart the flame of passion for you and help me walk in total obedience to your Word. I want to be your faithful worker. Please provide me with the strength I need to do the work I so desire to do for you. Help me now, using the gifts you have given me, to begin and complete the good works you have prepared in advance for me to do. I pray these things in the name of Jesus, the one who created me for good works, amen.

MOVING FORWARD:

- Write down the spiritual gifts and talents God has given you. If you are not sure what they are, talk to your pastor and close Christian friends and ask for their help and counsel.

- Now prayerfully ask God to give you a short list of good deeds you can do. Ask him to show you this list, which Scripture says he prepared in advance for you.
- Choose one good deed and ask the Lord to help you begin and complete it faithfully and in his strength and power.

Were you aware that God has good works for you to do and has prepared them in advance as part of his sovereign plan for you? What do you need in order to start doing these good works to bring him glory?

EIGHTY-SIX
STILL THE SAME

"Remember your Creator in the days of your youth,
before the days of trouble come."
— Ecclesiastes 12:1

However we choose to define *trouble*, it seems apparent that we are called to remember our Lord as we have known him in our brighter and more blissful days. I guess something happens to our hearts when we are faced with trouble. What I had never doubted before are now causes for question. What I had loved before are now merely things I give only passing thoughts about. Weariness and discouragement have left me "too tired to care," and the things I had felt motivated to accomplish are now heavy burdens that have been piled on high. For better or worse, my life has undoubtedly changed.

Trials and darkness may seem to be plaguing these present times in my life, but I must not forget that our unchanging, everlasting God is still the same as he was yesterday, last year, or a thousand years ago, through sunny days and ones pouring with rain. My circumstances may lure me to think that the God who had so lovingly walked with me through gardens of peace and hills of joy has now become indifferent to the sorrows and pain in my life. But that is far from the truth. One thing I know and am deeply reassured by is this: trouble does not separate us from the love of God. I may feel robbed of joy and emptied of peace, but God is still loving me the way he always has. So I *would* do well to remember just *who* my creator was, is, and forever will be. He is holy, full of compassion, gracious, righteous, merciful, faithful, patient, kind . . .

PRAYER

Dear Lord,
Help me remember the days before many of my mental health problems became evident. You, my creator, were the same then as you are now: loving, caring, gracious, merciful, and full of compassion. You walked with me through gardens of peace and hills of joy, but now I feel like you have become indifferent to the sorrows and pain in my life. I am wrong. Please forgive me for not believing and trusting you in every season of my life, especially in my suffering. Remind me today that your love for me is unchanging and everlasting; that my illness and troubles can never separate me from your love; that I can depend on your love for me even in the darkest hours of my depression and anxiety, emotional pain and loneliness, fears and tears, or suicidal thoughts and harmful behaviour. I pray these things in the name of my creator, Jesus, whose love for me is everlasting, amen.

MOVING FORWARD:

- Write down three to five reasons why you believed God loved you when you did not suffer from any significant mental illness. Were these reasons consistent with Scripture, or just based on your own feelings?

- Now write down three to five reasons why you sometimes doubt God's love for you now, during times of significant mental health struggles. Are these reasons consistent with Scripture, or just based on your own feelings?
- Finally, write down three to five reasons why you know God loves you now, no matter how unmanageable or significant your symptoms currently may be.

What makes it hard for you to believe that the difficult circumstances in your life are part of your creator's plan to benefit you and that he will love you through every high and low with his steadfast love?

EIGHTY-SEVEN
MY GREATEST FEAR

"Now all has been heard; here is the conclusion of the matter: Fear God and keep his commandments, for this is the whole duty of man."

— Ecclesiastes 12:13

Fear can be a strong motivator for our actions. As I reflect on my various behaviors, I find that many of them are largely motivated by fear: fear of weight gain, fear of loss of control, fear of ridicule, fear of teasing, fear of disapproval, fear of negative judgment. Prompted by such fears, I engage in some rather harmful behaviors that are perhaps reflective of my desperate attempts to prevent those fears from being realized. Yes, intense fears can lead us to take extreme actions and measures, yet having a healthy fear of "appropriate" things that deserve our fear is beneficial and even *necessary* for us.

"Fear God and keep his commandments" (Ecclesiastes 12:13). Sometimes I wonder if I fear men more than I fear the Lord. Am I more motivated to obey the commands of God out of my fear of his holiness and awesomeness, or am I more concerned with doing the things that find favor in the eyes of men? Is my heart more grieved when I have sinned and fallen short of the glory of the Lord, or am I more deeply affected by the disapproval or anger of men? At the end of the day, the only one to whom we are held accountable is the only sovereign God. It is him whom we have ultimate responsibility to obey, and it is him who has the power to judge our thoughts, actions, and words. To fear anything or anyone else above God is foolish, for there is none higher than him, none more worthy, and none more deserving of our devotion, obedience, fear, and allegiance. We do not need to be consumed by worldly fears that choke, bind, and paralyze us, but let us fear our strong, powerful, and loving God, for when we fear him, there is nothing else for us to fear.

PRAYER

Dear God,

I am afraid of many things in life: fear of weight gain, fear of loss of control, fear of ridicule, fear of teasing, fear of bullying, fear of disapproval, and fear of negative judgment. I acknowledge that I often fear people more than I fear you. I am often more deeply affected by the disapproval and anger of my family, friends, co-workers, and fellow Christians than you, my God. Please forgive me, Lord. Help me live out my fear of you by keeping your commandments and obeying your will fully. You deserve my devotion, obedience, fear, and allegiance. You are the one who judges my thoughts, actions, and words. Help me to lay down the burden of my fears at your feet, and please replace my earthly fears with a healthy and respectful fear of you. For when I fear you, there is nothing else for me to fear. I pray this in the name of my awesome and powerful God, Jesus, who will judge the world, amen.

MOVING FORWARD:

- List three to five things you are most fearful of, in order of importance to you.

- Now place God on the top of that list.
- Write out the following verse on paper and read it every night for the next week: "There is no fear in love, but perfect love drives out fear. For fear has to do with punishment, the one who fears is not made perfect in love" (1 John 4:18).
- Remind yourself that a reverent fear of and love for God, motivated by respect and awe of his greatness and love, will help alleviate your fears of the things of the world.
- Memorize the phrase "*perfect love casts out fear.*"

Why do you think that your fears can be overcome by loving God and people more?

EIGHTY-EIGHT
DON'T LOSE ME

"Having believed, you were marked in him with a seal, the promised Holy Spirit, who is a deposit guaranteeing our inheritance until the redemption of those who are God's possession—to the praise of his glory."

— Ephesians 1:13-14

We are God's possession. We are *his*. What do we do with our possessions, the things that belong to us? We *treasure* them. We *value* them. We strive to *protect* them. How much more does God do so with us? I remember back in elementary school, we were required to label all our belongings with our names, from pencils to calculators to notebooks to gym clothes. While this was done to ensure that anything that became lost could be more easily found and identified, God marks us with his Spirit to guarantee the final redemption of us who are in him.

Sometimes it seems so difficult to carry on this fight

day after day. When wound upon wound are inflict-ed, and bucket after bucket of tears are shed, simply getting up to face a new morning proves to be much more challenging than I could have imagined. But I *cannot* give up; I *must not* despair. There is a "label" on me that gives me more than sufficient hope to sustain me through all trials I will ever endure. Jesus Christ has conquered it *all*—the pain, the abandonment, the sorrows, the desperation, and death itself. He has done all this so that you and I could be secured an eternal place to live with our Heavenly Father. That promised final day will come. It *will*. There *is* a guar-anteed eternal future for us with *no* pain, *no* abandon-ment, *no* sorrows, *no* hurts—this is the future we have to look forward to. I *cannot* quit, for I must "press on to take hold of that for which Christ Jesus took hold of me" (Philippians 3:12). Just hold on, and know that our faithful God will never fail or disappoint us.

PRAYER

Dear God,

Thank you that I am your possession. I belong to you. You have given me the Holy Spirit who is the seal that guarantees my inheritance until you come to take me home to heaven. I am finding each day more challenging than I could have imagined, as wound upon wound are inflicted, and bucket after bucket of tears are shed. Please forgive me for forgetting that your Holy Spirit is with me, helping me, guiding me, and comforting me, every day and every moment, until Christ returns for me. I am eagerly waiting for that day when there will be no pain, no abandonment, no sorrow, and no hurts. Help me not to quit but to press on to take hold of that for which Christ Jesus took hold of me. I pray this in the saving name of Jesus, the one who guarantees my salvation, amen.

MOVING FORWARD:

- Write down the following three items God *guarantees* every believer who receives Jesus as Lord and Savior through faith and repentance:

- The Holy Spirit (Ephesians 1:13-14)
  - Eternal life with Christ in heaven (John 3:16)
  - Pain and suffering on this earth, as he sanctifies us, in preparation for eternal life where we will be glorified with him (Romans 8:16-17)
- Meditate on the word "guarantee"; study its definition from a dictionary.
- If you struggle to remember that you belong to Jesus, consider setting an alarm on your phone several times a day with this message: "I am God's precious child, and I belong to him. He has guaranteed me a glorious, eternal inheritance."

Do you have peace in your heart knowing that it is Jesus who has given you the guarantee of the Holy Spirit? What makes you convinced that Jesus never breaks his promises?

EIGHTY-NINE
NEVER POWERLESS

"I pray also that the eyes of your heart may be enlightened in order that you may know. . . his incomparable great power for us who believe. That power is the same as the mighty strength he exerted when he raised Christ from the dead and seated him at his right hand in the heavenly realms."

— Ephesians 1:18-19

What amazing power is for us and at work in us who believe. The power of God that raised our Lord Jesus from the dead, *that* is the power that we have in him. How can we ever grasp this magnificent truth? No wonder Jesus said that mountains can be moved, and a tree can be uprooted and replanted if we have but faith like a mustard seed. Just imagine the tremendous power in us.

And how, exactly, are we to put this power to good use? Are our hearts open to understanding and appreciating this tremendous gift? Are we ready to see the astonishing things God can do in us when we come before him with receptive and humble hearts? There are periods in my life when I especially long to *witness* the power of God at work, praying day after day and night after night for the Lord to demonstrate his power in my life so that I can *see* the wonders that come from his strong hand. In times when I feel so weak and helpless, I need to be reminded that the One who holds all the power in the world is presently strengthening me, supporting me, building me up, and protecting me. If the power of God raised our Lord Jesus from the *dead*, he can surely raise me up from these deep valleys and raging seas of pain. He is the solid rock upon which my feet are firmly and unshakably planted, so let me simply believe that his all-surpassing power is able to keep me firm and secure within even the most tempestuous storms of life.

PRAYER

Dear God,

Thank you for Christ's death and resurrection. Thank you that the same power that raised Jesus from the dead is working in me through Christ. Please forgive me for not understanding and appreciating this truth and not making use of your power in my weaknesses, especially when I struggle through my depression, anxiety, and destructive behavior. Remind me every day that you are the One who holds all the power in the world, and by that same power, you are strengthening me, supporting me, building me up, and protecting me. I come to you today with an open and humble heart, longing to witness your power working in me and through me. May your power keep me firm and secure in my faith in Christ and in my obedience to your Word, even in the deep valleys and raging storms of my pain. I pray these things in the powerful name of Jesus, the One who is seated at the right hand of the Heavenly Father, in the heavenly realms, amen.

MOVING FORWARD:

- Make a poster with one of the following truths

written on it:

The power of God in me is a free gift of God given to me by faith.

The power of God that raised Jesus from the dead will raise me out of my illness.

- Hang the poster on a wall where you can read it daily.

In what and whom do you draw power from—God's power, your own strengths and abilities, or something else?

NINETY
REVIVE THE FLAME

"For it is by grace you have been saved, through faith—and this not from yourselves, it is the gift of God – not by works, so that no one can boast."

— Ephesians 2:8-9

I went through a period in which I gave God the "cold shoulder." Reading his Word became a routine I merely went through every day. Praying also became only a ritual I practiced. In the morning, I would give a quarter-hearted word of thanks for a new day, and at night, I would reluctantly thank God for bringing me through another day. My mealtime prayers were most difficult to "forge" because not only did I not feel thankful for his provision of food, my deep fear, but I also didn't want God to bless the food because I wished I could dispose of it somehow.

As I began to pray for God to create in me a deep thirst and longing for him, he reinforced in me the truth that faith is, and has always been, a gift from him. Although I did not experience vivid encounters with the Lord throughout this time of dryness, he enabled me to continue trusting that he was still that same God I had come to know over the years.

Not only has God saved me from eternal condemnation and freely given me eternal life; he will also save me from every failure, hurt, and heartache I experience in this present life.

PRAYER

Dear God,

Am I giving you the "cold shoulder"? Is my present worship of Christ and service in your church simply a religious ritual, or is it my deep passion? Are the thanks I give you in my prayers coming from a heart of true gratitude, or are they just lip service? Search my heart and show me my errors in attitude, thoughts, and actions. Please forgive me where I have sinned. Create in me a deep thirst and longing for you, and reinforce the truth that faith has always been a gift from you. You have saved me from eternal condemnation and given me eternal life as a gift. I have been saved by faith, and only by faith, in Jesus Christ. Now I pray that you also save me from every failure, hurt, and heartache I experience in this present life. I pray these things in the saving name of Jesus, the giver of faith and eternal life, amen.

MOVING FORWARD:

- Circle *one* word from the four choices that expresses your present attitude toward each activity.

Bible reading	Burden	Ritual	Pleasure	Passion
Prayer	Burden	Ritual	Pleasure	Passion
Worship	Burden	Ritual	Pleasure	Passion
Giving thanks	Burden	Ritual	Pleasure	Passion

- If your answers are not "pleasure" or "passion," ask the Lord to change your heart and ignite in you a deep passion for him.

Have you accepted Jesus into your life as Lord and Savior by faith, with true repentance and complete surrender to him? Which of the disciplines listed above do you need to focus on nurturing to help you grow in your faith journey?

NINETY-ONE
YOU WANT TO HEAR FROM ME?

"And pray in the Spirit on all occasions with all kinds of prayers and requests."

— Ephesians 6:18

We aren't told to *only* pray about things we're uncertain of, things we're afraid of, or things we need. Of course, these are all things we should pray about, but we are called to pray on *all* occasions with *all* kinds of prayers and requests.

There are times when I think I don't "need" to pray because I feel like certain things would happen anyway regardless of whether or not I prayed. If I feel confident about and studied hard for an exam, for example, then I don't need to pray about it because I would certainly do well . . . right? If wonderful opportunities and good things effortlessly land in my lap, then clearly, they must be within the will of God, and thus, I need not pray about them . . . right? But would God bless us and shower us with tremendous grace so that we would drift *away* from him rather than draw near to him? If we stop praying, is this not what we are essentially doing? Are we not now at great risk of becoming self-reliant rather than God-reliant?

Yes, God is one who rescues us in times of heartaches and trials, but he is also one who longs to walk *with* us every single step of the way—across mountains of joy and through valleys of pain. As the psalmist said, "Yet I am always with you; you hold me by my right hand" (Psalm 73:23). We cannot imagine the immense grace of God in our lives. "He performs wonders that cannot be fathomed, miracles that cannot be counted" (Job 5:9). The things we are able to thank him for are likely to be only a tiny portion of his abundant blessings toward us. No, the good things that happen in our lives don't happen because they *should*; they happen because God chooses to love us and save us from the wrath we truly deserve. God loves to hear from us, so let us pray, and let us pray continually.

PRAYER

Dear Lord,

Thank you for the reminder to pray on all occasions with all kinds of prayers and requests. Forgive me for often neglecting prayer. I claim to believe in prayer, but my actions do not always reflect that. My faith in prayer is weak, and my devotion to prayer is even weaker. Your Word teaches me that you want me to pray for my good; you command me to pray for my benefit; you allow me to pray for my joy; you answer my prayers for my present and future well-being, as well as for your glory. Help me to show you how much I love you and others through regular prayer. As I go through my current struggles, I want to show you my full dependence on you by praying daily for your will to be done in my life. I want to bring you glory through prayer as I worship you, thank and praise you, confess my sins to you, and ask you to provide for my needs. I pray these things in the name of Jesus, my prayer advocate, amen.

MOVING FORWARD:

- Learn to make prayer part of your daily lifestyle by including it in your regular activities.

Consider practicing some of the following suggestions:

- o Instead of listening to the radio or music in your car or on the bus or train, use that time to pray.
- o Pray every time you brush your teeth, shave, or take a shower.
- o Every time you say grace before each meal, spend thirty seconds confessing your sins.
- o Whenever you take your medications, pray a prayer of thanksgiving.
- o Worship and praise God in prayer every time you wash the dishes.

- To help you pray "all kinds of prayers," learn the common and fairly well-known acronym, A.C.T.S., which stands for Adoration, Confession, Thanksgiving, and Supplication.

What do you need to change in your life to make prayer a greater part of your daily activities?

NINETY-TWO
TO BE SOMEBODY ELSE

"You were taught, with regard to your former way of life, to put off your old self, which is being corrupted by its deceitful desires; to be made new in the attitude of your minds; and to put on the new self, created to be like God in true righteousness and holiness."

— Ephesians 4:22-24

I often wish I lived in another person's body, thinking that all the concerns I presently have regarding my own self and body would disappear if only I were in someone else's body. There are so many flawed, deficient, and imperfect aspects of myself that I want to sneak under the skin of someone else or somehow cut off all that is undesirable about me. But if I would just pause to consider the implications of what I believe I want. What gain is there to exchange my body of sin for yet another body of sin? Regardless of what our outward appearances may be like, every human being's flesh is corrupted by sin, corrupted by wickedness. God, the most perfect and righteous judge of all, looks not at outward appearances; he examines rather the contents of our hearts. Who are we to be so critical of this or that detail of our or others' physical appearances?

Let me not think of putting on another person's self, but let me focus instead on putting on the new self that is created for righteousness and holiness. Let me not be so concerned with transforming my body to please earthly eyes, but let me submit myself wholly to the Lord for the renewing of my mind. Yes, I have every reason to hate my old self, one that was left to perish in its sinfulness, but I must remember that "if anyone is in Christ, he is a new creation; the old has gone, the new has come!" (2 Corinthians 5:17). No matter how dissatisfied I may be with myself, I must remember that the only thing that can truly satisfy is not found in the "perfect" body of a fellow sinner. Christ Jesus, my Redeemer and Lord, has rescued me from my body of death, taking all my sins upon himself and dying to pay the price for all my imperfections. When God looks at me, he does not see a body not skinny enough or legs too short or the like; he sees his beautifully created child, precious and so deeply loved by him.

And so, I must keep pursuing this path of righteousness, continuing to marvel at God's magnificent, sanctifying work in me. "And we, who with unveiled faces all reflect the Lord's glory, are being transformed into his image with ever-increasing glory, which comes from the Lord, who is the Spirit" (2 Corinthians 3:18). I need not wish to be someone else because every day, I am becoming more and more like Jesus. Come now, what more could we possibly desire?

PRAYER

Dear God,

I do not like what I see in my body, which is corrupted in sin and wickedness. I am often focusing on another person's self, as I compare their bodies to mine. Please forgive me, and help me focus on putting on the new self that is created for righteousness and holiness. Give me courage and strength so that I am not concerned with transforming my body to please earthly eyes. Instead, let me submit myself wholly to you for the renewing of my mind. When I repented of my sins, and your Holy Spirit came into my soul, I became a new creation in Christ. I have been transformed to enjoy you and be totally satisfied in you. Each day, your work of sanctification in me does not create a perfect body, but it makes me more like Christ in character, as my thoughts, words, and actions resemble Christ's. Please transform my mind, and help me walk in righteousness and holiness. I pray this in the righteous and holy name of Jesus, amen.

MOVING FORWARD:

- Write down a list of five things you would like to change about your appearance. Ask the Lord to help you change the features that can be changed and put behind the ones that can't. Consult a trusted, mature friend or your doctor. Create a plan on how you can make the appropriate changes to your appearance if they are consistent with a life lived within God's will.
- Now make a list of the spiritual and character changes God needs to make in your life. Consult a close, mature friend or pastor if you are not sure what those changes are. Create a plan on how you can make the appropriate changes. Consider including frequent prayer, Bible reading, and regular church attendance.

When was the last time you saw yourself as a new creation in Christ? Do you need to be reminded that the transformation into a new creature took place at your conversion? Why or why not?

NINETY-THREE
THE POTENCY OF ANGER

"'In your anger do not sin': Do not let the sun go down while you are still angry."

— Ephesians 4:26

Just because I don't have a particularly loud voice, many people assume that I never become angry. They tell me they cannot imagine me being upset with anyone or cause anyone to become upset with me, and while I suppose these are compliments, I can only conclude that I must hide things really, really well. It is true that I had been relatively "tame" for much of my life and rarely ever became seriously angry, but perhaps this was only because nothing was so upsetting to me that a "little" tantrum could not cure. But ever since my present struggles began to emerge, I found myself becoming angry much more easily and quickly. Small issues that frustrated me would send me into a violent frenzy—doors would slam, floors would be stomped upon, walls would be beaten, papers would be torn, and even some of my most treasured belongings would get thrown around. An overwhelming urge to slap, hit, and wound would often seize my mind, overpowering the weak defenses that I try to put up to resist these temptations.

I am sure many of us have heard about how we should not allow our emotions to control us, but how much easier is that said than done? God has created us with emotions so that we can love and appreciate, empathize and sympathize, but how are we to handle such difficult, and perhaps even dangerous, emotions? A simple answer is that we must not sin. Each time I give into verbal or physical aggression in response to my anger, there is an element of relief mixed into the guilt and pain that I feel. As with all behaviors, sinful actions do accomplish some purpose, be it for pleasure, relief, satisfaction, or revenge. But as convenient and effective such behaviors may seem, God desires for us to refrain from sinning in order to achieve our goals.

There's not anything inherently "wrong" or "bad" about the emotion of anger itself, but what we must be careful about is how we act and react when we are provoked to anger. Not only do I greatly need God's wisdom to discern right from wrong, but I also desperately need the Lord to help me replace my hurtful and sinful actions with ones that please and honor him.

PRAYER

Dear Lord,
I sometimes have a problem controlling my anger. Your Word teaches me that anger itself is not a sin, but acting inappropriately because of the anger can be a sin. Please forgive me for my inappropriate behavior during my anger outbursts. Please teach me how to use my anger appropriately for good causes without sinning. Help me to control my emotions and to never engage in physical violence or verbal abuse. Give me godly wisdom to make the right choices when I am angry and provoked. I ask that the Holy Spirit help me replace my hurtful and sinful actions with ones that please and honor you. I pray this in the name of Jesus, the One who deals with me patiently and lovingly, amen.

MOVING FORWARD:

- Think of the last few times you were angry. How did you react? Consider the following two lists of actions and circle the ones you engaged in.
    - Shouting, swearing, threatening, hit-

ting, breaking or throwing objects, slamming doors, abusing drugs and alcohol, binge eating, slandering, focusing on past hurts, engaging in inappropriate sexual behavior, etc.

  - Giving time for your emotions to calm, spending time in quiet reflection, praying, asking God for wisdom to respond appropriately, providing a soft answer, repenting, seeking godly counsel from mature Christians, looking for wisdom in the Bible, talking through the issues with those involved in a mature manner, etc.

- Now ask the Lord to help you change your pattern of behavior to the suggestions in the second list.

If you struggle to manage your anger, who can you talk to about it? Can your doctor or pastor help you learn effective ways and skills to manage anger?

NINETY-FOUR
THE DANGER OF "JUST ONCE"

"Do not give the devil a foothold."

— Ephesians 4:27

I think back to the time when I was free from my incessant obsession over my weight and all that goes along with it. I remember not constantly feeling like an unloved individual who was left all alone because I felt that there were always people around me who truly loved me and cared for me. I remember not having to hurt myself in order to release feelings of anger, fright, frustration, or sadness. I remember not engaging in physically and emotionally exhausting behaviors that were unable to help me control anything. How did I get from there to here? There seems to have been so little warning.

I guess a "slow" fall does not necessarily mean a "safe" fall. I don't know if I can identify the actual triggers that first precipitated my feelings of loneliness and isolation, but I do know that the initial few instances of my harmful behaviors were certainly done in the deceiving mindset of "I'll only do this once." As time went on, and I became more "creative" and "skilled," I kept on with my false "no more tomorrow" thinking, only to find myself becoming more and more tightly bound to and reliant on my behaviors.

Do not give the devil a foothold. Let him slip and slide and fall, but don't let him find that crevice in your life where he can whisper and implant tantalizing lies. Don't walk up that mountain of false "just once's" because the devil will surely catch up with you along the way and eventually try to push you off it. If you're like me—dangerously near the top—please quickly sprint your way back down. "Resist the devil, and he will flee from you" (James 4:7). It is so much easier said than done, really. Having seen how much I have failed, I am afraid of imagining just how much further I can go. But I know that the Lord is the ultimate victor in this battle. He will give my heels the strength to dig down deep and resist the devil, and I know he will pry the devil away from the footholds he had gained, one day freeing me completely from all the chains that grip me so tightly and fiercely.

PRAYER

Dear God,

I have allowed the devil to gain a foothold in some areas of my life, and it's now causing me to sin on a regular basis. The temptations are becoming more difficult to overcome, and sinning is becoming more frequent. Please forgive me and cleanse me. Help me never to say, "I will do this sinful behavior only once." Teach me how to resist the devil so that he will flee from me. I have allowed myself to fall into sin during temptations, often during my depression and anxiety. I now seem to sin more freely and frequently because I have allowed the devil a strong foothold in my life. I am deeply sorry. Today I plead that you pry the devil away from the footholds he has gained, freeing me completely from all the chains that grip me so tightly and fiercely. I pray this in the victorious name of Jesus, amen.

MOVING FORWARD:

- List one or two areas of your life where you believe the devil has gained a foothold in your life.

- Think back to *when* that happened and *how* it may have happened.
- Confess your errors to the Lord and ask him for wisdom to replace any harmful behaviors with ones that honor and glorify him.
- Seek help from your pastor on what it means to "walk in the Spirit." Read Galatians 5:16-25 for context.

Have you ever considered declaring war on the devil by surrendering your life completely to Jesus? What would that look like on a daily basis?

NINETY-FIVE
BITING MY TONGUE

"Do not let any unwholesome talk come out of your mouths, but only what is helpful for building others up according to their needs, that it may benefit those who listen."

— Ephesians 4:29

Would you agree that *truth* can be conveyed in a number of ways? It can be told in a harsh and critical tone, with little sensitivity to how the recipient may react or interpret the speaker's intent. Or it can be said with gentleness and genuine concern, with the sole motive of edifying and benefitting the one who hears. In no way do I suggest that we should euphemize truths to make them more palatable for others, but can we not make sure that we always speak out of love and try not to destroy the faith of our brothers and sisters?

We must speak the truth, but if we do so with the intention of judging and disparaging people for their sins, perhaps we would do well to hold our tongues. It is the Lord who judges: "Therefore judge nothing before the appointed time; wait till the Lord comes. He will bring to light what is hidden in darkness and will expose the motives of men's hearts" (1 Corinthians 4:5). There is no need for us to "help" the Lord get a head start on this task. Pointing out faults and shortcomings in other people can have the effect of increasing our own sense of self-righteousness, perhaps by way of "pushing others down to push ourselves up." We must begin to evaluate our true motivations for the words that come out of our mouths.

If we shift our focus off of ourselves and take heed of the specific needs we observe in others, the Lord can grant us wisdom to know when to speak and which words to use *when* we speak. Wholesome talk is that which fosters positive well-being and pushes one into the arms of Christ. When we keep this in mind, God can produce in us useful and edifying speech that is seasoned and enveloped with his grace and love.

PRAYER

Dear Lord,
Please help me evaluate what kind of talk comes out of my mouth. Is it language that is helpful in building others up, according to their needs, or are my words harsh and hurtful, discouraging and divisive, judgmental and condemning? Show me where I am sinning, and please let your Holy Spirit guide me to speak words that benefit those who listen. I repent of my sinful words and my sinful attitude. Forgive me for pointing out faults and shortcomings in other people in order to increase my own self-righteousness. Help me never to use my mental health problems as an excuse to use harmful language. I pray that as I walk in the Spirit, you will help me choose wholesome talk and edifying speech that is seasoned and enveloped in your grace and love. I pray these things in the name of Jesus, the Word of Life, amen.

MOVING FORWARD:

- List two or three common situations when you often use hurtful language or harmful words.
- Identify several quick prayers you can speak to

replace harmful words you may normally use.

- Ask God to transform your mind in order to transform your speech.
- Read Romans 12:1-2.

What aspects of your speech need to be transformed during your times of significant mental health struggles? Can you change your behaviour during those times by calling out to God for help? What would that look like?

NINETY-SIX
SHOW ME YOU UNDERSTAND

"Be kind and compassionate to one another."

— Ephesians 4:32

I wish that people would understand. If they would only understand just how difficult this all is. If they would simply understand how it can be so hard to simply get out of bed and *do* the most basic of things, then maybe they would stop asking questions that only frustrate me and pestering me with questions I do not want to answer. If they would only understand, then perhaps they would be able to empathize with me rather than unrelentingly heap upon me hurtful words and actions.

I do not mean to accuse or blame anybody for my pain, but I do believe that these experiences invite me to evaluate my own ways of treating people around me. Having known so intimately the sting of being responded to with seemingly little consideration and gentleness, I wonder if, or to what extent, I act similarly to others.

Being kind and compassionate isn't easy, nor does it come naturally for us in many circumstances. It can be tempting to defend unloving acts by validating our own hurts, for after all, how can anyone expect us to treat others with kindness if we are in such deep pain ourselves? Well if this is the case, then how can we expect *others* to love us with care and concern? "Do to others as you would have them do to you" (Luke 6:31). We are all familiar with this, yet how often do we long for others to do to us what we are unwilling to do ourselves? Be kind and compassionate to others no matter how hard it may prove and how much we may seem to lose, for this is what God wills for us. "Therefore, as God's chosen people, holy and dearly loved, clothe yourselves with compassion, kindness, humility, gentleness and patience. Bear with each other and forgive one another if any of you has a grievance against someone. Forgive as the Lord forgave you" (Colossians 3:12-13).

PRAYER

Dear Lord,

I am in emotional pain and turmoil, and I need people to deal with me kindly and compassionately. I desire to have you and those around me pour compassion, kindness, and gentleness on me, forgiving all my grievances. Yet this word reminds me that I need to be kind and compassionate to others too, doing to them what I would have them do to me. Please forgive me where I have not shown compassion and kindness, especially to those suffering from mental health problems like me. As I struggle in my own pain, I often fail to see how many others are suffering from various other mental health problems. Please pour your Holy Spirit into me and use me, your chosen child, holy and dearly loved, to share the compassion and kindness of Christ with those who are dearly loved by you. Remind me also that you understand all of my deepest sorrows and pain, and you, in your love and mercy, will help me be loving and merciful to those around me. I ask these things in the loving and compassionate name of Christ, amen.

MOVING FORWARD:

- Make a list of people who have shown you

kindness and compassion in the last few years. Take some time and effort to thank them and God.

- Now make a list of people who today need to receive some kindness and compassion from you. Take some time and effort to plan how you can do that.
- Ask the Lord for an extra measure of his compassion and kindness to you today.

Are you willing to forgive others as the Lord has forgiven you? Are you willing to show compassion and kindness to others as the Lord shows compassion and kindness to you? What steps can you begin to take today in order to do just that?

NINETY-SEVEN
JUST LIKE YOU

"Be imitators of God."

— Ephesians 5:1

Imitating God. Doesn't that seem a little too difficult for us to even attempt? But then again, Jesus himself taught us to be perfect as our heavenly Father is perfect (Matthew 5:48). Is that even possible? Haven't we all been told that "nobody is perfect"? If so, why bother putting in the effort to try?

Just because we cannot accomplish perfection on our own does not mean we should not commit ourselves to striving to follow the ways of God in all we do. The image that comes to my mind is that of a young child first learning how to write. As she tries to imitate her teacher's perfectly proportionate and neat printing with her own large and sometimes inverted letters, the child does not merely give up and quit. Over time, with much practice and patient guidance from her teacher, the child's writing becomes more refined and even begins to resemble "adult writing." In a similar way, our growth in holiness is a process that takes time, perseverance, and determination. Just like a teacher who grasps a child's hand to guide and direct her movements, the Holy Spirit that resides in us is leading us and helping us each moment to become more and more like Christ.

Although we may be desperately falling short in many areas of our lives, we must fervently and diligently draw near to our perfect God to truly learn from the Master. No matter how many times we may fall or how frustrated and discouraged we may become, we must continue striving to live a life that beautifully glorifies our God, for this is the highest calling we must pursue. Offer your whole self to God and allow him to shape you as a potter does his clay. This road of sanctification can be the most exciting and satisfying journey of all, and even if changes don't take place over night, know that God is molding you into someone more beautiful than you can ever imagine or hope to be.

PRAYER

Dear God,

Thank you for being the perfect example of who I need to become. You call me not to be "better," but to be "perfect." In my struggles with my mental health problems, I have given up trying to be better, let alone perfect. I thank you for working in me every day, causing me to grow in holiness. Your Holy Spirit is personally involved in my life as my Master and potter, taking me down an exciting journey, molding me into someone more beautiful than I could ever imagine. Thank you that your standard for who you want me to be is very high because your love for me is very great. My mental health problems are not a hindrance in the process of making me perfect, but an instrument in your hands. Today I fully surrender to your will and plan for my life and accept the process of sanctification with thanksgiving. I pray these things in the name of Jesus, my Master, amen.

MOVING FORWARD:

- Consider the following list of tools and instruments God uses to sanctify people:

- Our family members, people who don't like us and/or disagree with us, teachers, difficulties related to our children, our closest friends.
- Physical and mental illnesses, financial difficulties, unemployment, persecution, the illnesses or death of family and friends, pain, loneliness.
- Government, laws, injustice.
- The Bible, good Christian books

- Can you think of any others?
- Which of these is God using presently in your life?

Which instruments of God's sanctification do you usually accept with ease, and which ones do you tend to resist?

NINETY-EIGHT
YEARNING FOR LOVE

"Live a life of love, just as Christ loved us and gave himself up for us as a fragrant offering and sacrifice to God."

— Ephesians 5:2

I feel this deep desire in me for someone to love me more than anything else they may have and any other person they may know. I long so much to be most important and special to somebody, to be especially cherished and loved by even just one person. I suppose I feel that if there was just one person who truly needed me and depended on me for *something*, I might not feel as neglected, useless, and dispensable as I do now.

As I ponder upon the perfect love of God for us, I somehow find myself still unsatisfied. I guess my wish to be "especially" loved doesn't seem to be fulfilled by the love of God because after all, he died for *everyone,* and he loves *everyone*, not only me. But if I consider the fact that God who *is* love gave *all* of himself for each one of us, and that he cannot love us "more" than he already does because his love for us is already infinite and eternal, I must begin to grasp just how special I am in his eyes. And this is the wonder of God's love, isn't it? That he is able to love every single person "most" by his perfect, unmatchable love. Perhaps I should stop trying to calculate the magnitudes and degrees of people's love for me, but rather devote myself to the task of imitating the selfless, complete love that my God demonstrates toward us.

We, as human beings, cannot love with the perfect love of God, nor should we expect to receive that kind of love from others. People can only give so much of themselves to us, so when they don't give their whole selves for us, we truly should simply feel blessed by what they *are* willing and able to give, rather than focus on what we seem to lack in our relationships with them. Christ died for us not because we loved him, however much or little, so we should love others regardless of what we seem to receive in return. May the love we show bring glory and honor to God, rising to him as a fragrant offering and willing sacrifice to our ever-loving God.

PRAYER

Dear God,

Thank you for loving me perfectly with sacrificial love. Your love for me is unconditional and everlasting. It was there before I was even born, and it will remain into eternity. You took the punishment of my sins upon yourself and died for me, gave me the gift of eternal life, and promised me your fellowship and friendship forever. I know you love me, but I just don't always feel it. Please forgive me for sometimes doubting your love, as I often evaluate it by my own feelings. Help me to enjoy you every day: your kindness, grace, mercy, peace, comfort, provision of food, clothing, a home, transportation, money, your Word, a church, friends, family, medication, healthcare, education, your beautiful creation, and so much more. Help me to grasp how special I am in your eternal plan for all of creation. Now encourage me to be an imitator of Christ, living a life of love. I pray this in the loving name of Jesus, the love of my life, amen.

MOVING FORWARD:

- Write down a list of things that make you feel

loved. Examples may include physical affection, receiving gifts, getting help from others, hearing words of affirmation, and people spending time with you.[5]

- Now write a list of *when* you feel loved by God. In other words, what does God have to do for you in order for you to feel loved?
- Compare the two lists. Are they similar or very different?

How much do you believe the truth that God does more for you and loves you more than any person ever has or will? Is this enough for you?

NINETY-NINE
EQUIPPED FOR BATTLE

"Therefore put on the full armor of God, so that when the day of evil comes, you may be able to stand your ground, and after you have done everything, to stand."

— Ephesians 6:13

Standing is not as easy as it sounds. Think of the baby who is just learning to hold himself up with his two wobbly legs or the victim of a car accident that has left him with broken and injured limbs. Even for us "seasoned stand-ers," keeping ourselves upright in the midst of a vicious windstorm can prove to be extremely difficult, if not impossible. Or how about severe earthquakes and other catastrophes that literally pull the ground out from beneath our feet? No, the simple act of standing can indeed be a great challenge.

The destructive and luring schemes of Satan are undoubtedly much more powerful and destructive than unfortunate circumstances or dangerous weather, yet God has equipped us with more than flimsy umbrellas and plastic raincoats to withstand Satan's attacks: he has given us the full armor of God. In every battle we find ourselves in, the Lord provides us with: his *truth* to counter and expose every one of Satan's lies, his *righteousness* that is ours through the sinless life Christ sacrificed on our behalf, his *peace* that settles and appeases all our worries and anxieties, his *faith* that allows us to endure, trust, and obey, his gift of *salvation* that gives us immovable hope and eternal security, and the flawless *Word of God* that is our perfect guide and source of all wisdom and power. In the Lord, we are definitely more than ready to stand strong in this war against Satan. So let us not be afraid to stand, for we always have on us the unconquerable, invincible protection of God.

PRAYER

Dear God,

The powerful and destructive schemes of the devil surround me every day. As I struggle with my mental health difficulties, I feel Satan tempting me, discouraging me, and roaring at me in order to see me hurt and fall. Yet, I know I have you, and with you, I have available to me the full armor of God. Your armor is designed and custom-made to fit me perfectly. It is indestructible, not a burden, and instantly available to me. You give it to me as a gift, and you even help me put it on. Once it is on, I never need to take it off. Today I pray that you help me put on your full armor, leaving no piece behind. Please forgive me for going into spiritual battle without some of the armor you gave me. I will now take your truth to counter and expose every one of Satan's lies. I will hold fast to God's righteousness that is mine through the sinless life Christ sacrificed on my behalf. I will rely on your peace that settles and appeases all my worries and anxieties. I will receive your faith that allows me to endure, trust, and obey and your gift of salvation that gives me immovable hope and eternal security. Finally, I will depend on the flawless Word of God that is my perfect guide and source of all wisdom and power. I pray these things in the powerful name of Christ, amen.

MOVING FORWARD:

- Review God's armor, which is provided and custom-made for you (Ephesians 6:14-18):
    - Belt of truth.
    - Breastplate of righteousness.
    - Gospel of peace.
    - Shield of faith
    - Helmet of salvation.
    - Sword of the Spirit.

  Which of these have you *not* put on? Ask the Lord to help you put on his *full* armor so that you can stand against the schemes of the evil one.

Which aspects of God's armor are you wearing today?

ONE HUNDRED
DESPERATE FOR FAITH

"Without faith it is impossible to please God, because anyone who comes to him must believe that he exists and that he rewards those who earnestly seek him."

— Hebrews 11:6

Someone once said that "faith is the capacity to keep going between Good Friday and Easter Sunrise."[6] If *faith* is "being sure of what we hope for and certain of what we do not see" (Hebrews 11:1), then it is certainly the very thing we need to get us through the darkest times. From death to life, we must trust. From utter despair and resurrected hope, we must trust. From doubt to certainty, we must trust.

We can be bold and confident in our faith because the One in whom we place our trust is the very God who holds our promised reward in his self-sustaining and all-sustaining hands. He is forever faithful to his beloved children, and no "external factor" or "unforeseen circumstance" can ever foil his plans to secure a perfect future for his blood-bought children. Faith isn't about comprehending every one of God's actions or understanding his every motivation; it is about receiving the hope he offers to fill our hearts, and it's about pursuing and relying on that hope regardless of how unlikely or impossible his promises may seem. It is only in God that the outcomes of our faith can be realized, so we *must* seek the Lord earnestly. His desire for the security of our hearts and souls is so strong that he chooses *himself*, the unchanging and everlasting Rock, to be our only dependable source of hope. Whatever else we may strive to build our assurance upon will surely fail and disappoint us, but let us hold fast to our Lord and courageously place our complete faith in him. "[L]et us hold unswervingly to the hope we profess, for he who promised is faithful" (Hebrews 10:23).

PRAYER

Dear God,

Thank you for giving me the faith to believe that you exist and that you reward me for earnestly seeking you. Please help me to trust you for the things that I do not see at this time, such as the restoration of my mental health, control over my anxiety and fears, relief of the pain from any past abuse, and freedom from the torment of my addictions. I want to trust you, but I can't do it without you. I want to have sufficient faith in you in order to get me through the darkest times when the joy and peace that I hope for are out of sight and seem so far out of reach. Thank you for teaching me that faith in you comes from you and from reading and understanding your Word. Convince me today that I must seek you earnestly in order for the outcomes of my life to be realized. You, and only you, are the source of my hope, my trust, and my faith. All else will surely fail and disappoint me. I pray this in the name of Jesus, my rock, my foundation, and the source of my faith, amen.

MOVING FORWARD:

- Underline in your Bible the phrase "he rewards those who earnestly seek him" from today's Scripture, Hebrews 11:6. Then highlight the word "earnestly."

- Look up the meaning of the word "earnestly" in a dictionary and thesaurus. Consider words such as "seriously," "intently," "fervently," "eagerly," and phrases such as "showing sincere and intense conviction."[7]
- Ask yourself, "Is this how I am seeking my Lord Jesus?"

In what ways have you found reading the Bible to be instrumental in helping your faith grow?

ONE HUNDRED AND ONE
THIS HOPE SHALL REMAIN

"May our Lord Jesus Christ himself and God our Father, who loved us and by his grace gave us eternal encouragement and good hope, encourage your hearts and strengthen you in every good deed and word."

— 2 Thessalonians 2:16-17

Hope is not situational, varying in certainty and dependability with differing circumstances. It is precisely because of its unchanging nature that hope is able to sustain us and carry us through even the stormiest and darkest times in our lives. The hope that we profess and hold onto—that Christ Jesus our Lord has died and risen again to secure for us eternal life with the living God—this is what encourages us and allows us to persevere through all circumstances. This hope is what allows us to take hold of that ultimate prize we long and thirst for.

Although these reasons for hope are sufficient to sustain us through all of life's situations, sometimes the end seems a little too far away. I am so thankful that the Lord knows and understands this. We may become weary of speaking edifying and comforting words to hurting individuals, but he can provide us with the patience to continue speaking in love. We may become disappointed by not yet seeing the victorious outcomes of our struggles to remain obedient to the Lord, but he will give us the strength we need to keep walking those heavy steps of faith. No matter how tired we may feel from striving to please and live for the Lord without experiencing the rewards and outcomes we think we deserve, we do not need to worry about losing the desire or ability to do good, for God himself will encourage and strengthen us in every single good deed we do and in every good word we say. We may think that he is asking "too much" of us when he calls us to lay down our lives and follow him, but we can remember that he will give us the courage to live in and by faith, the strength to continue fighting, and the great anticipation of the glorious eternity that awaits us.

PRAYER

Dear Lord,

You have loved me, and by your grace, have given me eternal encouragement and good hope. However, today I need an extra measure of your grace, encouragement, good hope, and strength. I am traveling through some of the stormiest and darkest times of my life. My present situation has discouraged me, and I feel I am losing hope. Jesus, I believe that you have died and risen for me, securing eternal life for me. However, today I am disappointed by not seeing victorious outcomes as I struggle to remain obedient to you. Lord, please help me today to do good works and speak good words, to love and help others who are also hurting and discouraged. As I obey you in each of these acts of obedience, may your promise of eternal encouragement and hope increase in my life, and may I truly experience these blessings today. I pray these things in the encouraging name of Jesus, amen.

MOVING FORWARD:

- Think of one good deed you could do today. For example, consider giving your time to help a single mother or an elderly person, visiting a widow or someone who is sick in the hospital, making a financial donation to a mission or charity, babysitting for a tired friend or mowing the lawn of an elderly couple, or writing a note of encouragement to a struggling friend or family member. As you do the good deed, speak words of encouragement to those you are helping. Then watch and see how God encourages your heart and strengthens you as he answers your prayers today.

How can you commit to mind today's Scripture—2 Thessalonians 2:16-17? It promises us that Jesus loves us, and by his grace, he has given us eternal encouragement and hope.

OUR CLOSING PRAYER FOR YOU

Dear Heavenly Father,

Thank you for carrying your adopted and beloved children through the journey of reading this book. We pray that the Scriptures that have been read, the counsel that has been shared, the prayers that have been prayed, the questions that have been asked, and the steps that have been taken draw our readers closer to you and transform them in impactful and healing ways. We thank you for your perfect love and care for each believer who puts their trust in you and for reminding us of your faithfulness, goodness, kindness, mercy, and grace. We are believing in your power to heal your beloved children, and we ask that you grant them the strength they need to seek and follow you every moment of every day. May your grace overflow in their lives, reminding them that your special blessings are never far away and can be found in Jesus Christ alone. No matter how intense their mental illness may become, may they continue to persevere and hold tightly to your good promises. Surround your children from all sides, protect them from evil, and give them your power to stand firm in the face of all trials and temptation. Use each of your children even in their weaknesses and illnesses, and may your beauty shine through them for your glorious purposes. May you keep and bless your chosen people, make your face shine upon them, be gracious to each of them, turn your face toward them, and grant them peace. May we all be overwhelmed again by you, oh Lord, our Savior and our King. We love you and give all our praise and thanks to you. In the eternal, saving name of Jesus we pray, amen.

Dr. Peter Golin is the son of Russian refugees who fled the former Soviet Union to live in China for over twenty years before settling in Australia as new immigrants. He grew up in a Christian home with God-fearing parents and committed himself to the Lord at the age of fifteen. Dr. Golin graduated from the University of British Columbia, Canada, with a BS in Biochemistry, Teacher Training, and MD. He has been working as a medical doctor for thirty years, caring for the young and old and treating their physical, mental, and spiritual health. Dr. Golin has also served as a volunteer pastor, elder, and church leader for over thirty years. Using his spiritual gifts of preaching, teaching, shepherding, and evangelism, he has pursued his passion of reaching the lost for Christ. He established CCRROSS Training Ministries, a Christian organization devoted to equipping all believers with simple tools for effective evangelism. He presently works as a family doctor and travels internationally, teaching from his book, *Living the Gospel*. Dr. Golin has been married to his wife, Natasha, for thirty years and has three sons who confess Jesus as Lord. He currently lives in Burnaby, British Columbia, Canada.

Dr. Winnie Chung was born in Hong Kong and moved to Canada in her elementary school years. She committed her life to the Lord as an early adolescent, and has been seeking to follow him closely ever since. Dr. Chung graduated from the University of British Columbia in Vancouver, British Columbia, with a BA in Psychology, and later earned her MA and PhD in Psychology from The Ohio State University in Columbus, Ohio. She completed her pre-doctoral internship at Boston Children's Hospital, and her post-doctoral fellowship at Children's Hospital of Orange County. She is a clinical psychologist who specializes in helping families with children and adolescents experiencing mental health difficulties and other medical concerns. Dr. Chung is grateful for the opportunities God provides to allow her to serve and love others, particularly those with mental health struggles, with the hope, comfort, peace, and encouragement that is found in our Lord Jesus Christ. She currently resides in British Columbia, Canada.

ENDNOTES:

1. CDC Report: *Mental Illness Surveillance Among Adults in the United States.*" Center for Disease Control and Prevention. https://www.cdc.gov/mentalhealthsurveillance/fact_sheet.html.
2. Lifeway Reseach. "Study of Acute Mental Illness and Christian Faith Research Report." http://lifewayresearch.com/wp-content/uploads/2014/09/Acute-Mental-Illness-and-Christian-Faith-Research-Report-1.pdf.
3. Piper, John. (1986). *Desiring God.* Colorado Springs, CO: Multnomah Books.
4. *Zondervan Prayer Devotional Bible.* Ben Patterson, gen. ed. (Grand Rapids, MI: Zondervan Corporation, 2004). Print.
5. Chapman, Gary. (2015). The five love languages: the secret to love that lasts. Chicago, IL: Northfield Publishing.
6. Jeremiah, David. (2016). *Your Daily Journey with God: 365 Daily Devotions*. Carol Stream, IL: Tyndale House Publishers, Inc.
7. "Earnestly." OED Online. Oxford University Press, March 2017. Web. 4 May 2017.

ACKNOWLEDGMENTS

We would like to sincerely thank each individual the Lord has placed on our paths during the development of this book and throughout the course of our lives. We are truly grateful for all who have loved us, encouraged us, guided us, and supported us. This book would not have been possible without our families' love and encouragement, our friends' wisdom and inspiration, and our patients' demonstrations of great courage and perseverance. We our indebted to each of our brothers and sisters in Christ who have fellowshipped with us, instructed us, and helped shape the growth of our faith in the Lord Jesus.

Above all, our greatest thanks are to our God, who has loved us with his everlasting love, rescued our souls from the dominion of darkness, and restored our broken selves to himself through the blood of Christ. We will never cease to marvel at God's willingness to make himself known through our imperfect beings, and we are deeply humbled to be his vessels used to minister to the broken and the lost, magnify his eternal glory, and lift high his wonderful name.

NOTES

NOTES

NOTES

NOTES

NOTES

NOTES

NOTES

NOTES

NOTES

NOTES

NOTES

NOTES